LOS ANGELES

From Pueblo to
City of the Future

Andrew Rolle

D0557901

series editors:
Norris Hundley, jr.
John A. Schutz

Boyd & Fraser Publishing Company
San Francisco

F
869
L8
R84

LOS ANGELES:
FROM PUEBLO TO CITY OF THE FUTURE

Andrew Rolle

© Copyright 1981 by Boyd & Fraser Publishing Company, 3627 Sacramento Street, San Francisco, CA 94118. All rights reserved.

No part of this work may be reproduced or used in any form or by any means—graphic, electronic, or mechanical including photocopying, recording, taping, or information and retrieval systems—without written permission from the publisher.

Manufactured in the United States of America.

Library of Congress catalog card number: 81-67252

ISBN 0-87835-119-1

5 4 3 2 1 · 5 4 3 2 1

EDITORS' INTRODUCTION

MENTION THE NAME CALIFORNIA and the popular mind conjures up images of romance and adventure of the sort that prompted the Spaniards in the 1540s to name the locale after a legendary Amazon queen. State of mind no less than geographic entity, California has become a popular image of a wonderful land of easy wealth, better health, pleasant living, and unlimited opportunities. While this has been true for some, for others it has been a land of disillusionment, and for too many it has become a place of crowded cities, congested roadways, smog, noise, racial unrest, and other problems. Still, the romantic image has persisted to make California the most populated state in the Union and the home of more newcomers each year than came during the first three hundred years following discovery by Europeans.

For most of its history California has been shrouded in mystery, better known for its terrain than for its settlers—first the Indians who arrived at least 11,000 years ago and then the Spaniards who followed in 1769. Spaniards, Mexicans, and blacks added only slightly to the non-Indian population until the American conquest of 1846 ushered in an era of unparalleled growth. With the discovery of gold, the building of the transcontinental railroad, and the development of crops and cities, people in massive numbers from all parts of the world began to inhabit the region. Thus California became a land of newcomers where a rich mixture of cultures pervades.

Fact and fiction are intertwined so well into the state's traditions and folklore that they are sometimes difficult to separate. But close scrutiny reveals that the people of California have made many solid contributions in land and water use, conservation of resources, politics, education, transportation, labor organization, literature, architectural styles, and learning to live with people of different cultural and ethnic heritages. These contributions, as well as those instances when Californians performed less admirably, are woven into the design of the Golden

136059

State Series. The volumes in the Series are meant to be suggestive rather than exhaustive, interpretive rather than definitive. They invite the general public, the student, the scholar, and the teacher to read them not only for digested materials from a wide range of recent scholarship, but also for some new insights and ways of perceiving old problems. The Series, we trust, will be only the beginning of each reader's inquiry into the past of a state rich in historical excitement and significant in its impact on the nation.

Norris Hundley, jr.
John A. Schutz

*For Richard Lillard, whose personal Eden
has never been in jeopardy*

CONTENTS

CHAPTER ONE

City of the Angels: An Overview

LOS ANGELES provides a massive culture shock for those easterners who believe that life ends west of the Hudson River. Angelenos are sometimes portrayed by them as living on the outskirts of a vast wasteland, as persons of little couth, who are culturally vapid, tending toward a laid-back life spent in hot tubs. Little wonder, then, that the city is frequently seen as a center of vulgarity.

Such criticism of Los Angeles and of its residents is not new. In 1769 when the Franciscan padre Juan Crespi accompanied the Portolá party into the area, he described the inhabitants as "howling like wolves." In 1841, the English traveler Sir George Simpson called the sleepy pueblo a "den of thieves" and the "abode of the lowest drunkards and gamblers in the country." Over the years such acrid barbs against Los Angeles grew in number and variety. The epithets "Queen of the Cow Counties," the "Sea Coast of Iowa," and "Six Suburbs in Search of a City" are relatively mild disparagements. Comedian W. C. Fields called "L.A." a "Double Dubuque," while Sinclair Lewis labeled it "the retreat of all failures." Continuing to allege its vulgarity and fatuousness, the journalist Westbrook Pegler saw Los

Angeles as a "big, sprawling, incoherent, shapeless, slobbering idiot." Despite these slanders, the city has rolled with the punches, accepting the venom as though it were better to be criticized than to be ignored.[1]

Today the very size and power of Los Angeles seems to overwhelm its critics. Heart of the second most populous urbanized area in the United States, the city has attracted people from every part of the globe and has within its borders industry that is unique and diverse. The result is a city that dominates all of southern California which, in turn, is the most important part of the state in wealth, manufacturing, commerce, and transport.

This vast, sprawling megalopolis, which covers an area as large as Rhode Island, fans out in all directions. The city's most populated districts are bounded on the south and west by the Pacific Ocean. From its northeastern border Los Angeles extends seventy miles southward. Average elevation is 275 feet, falling between extremes of 5,080 feet, at the highest point, and sea level. Los Angeles, with its eighty-one adjoining municipalities and unincorporated suburbs, surrounds Beverly Hills and San Fernando. It bounds Culver City and Santa Monica on three sides and touches such cities as Pasadena and Long Beach. Hollywood, Glendale, and San Pedro are integral parts of Los Angeles. Many considerations prompted neighboring cities to seek annexation over the years, not the least being water which has always remained scarce.[2]

The city grew, too, because of its climate. Ironic remarks about Los Angeles weather are legion. One wag has stated that there are only two types of weather that afflict the city—perfect and unusual. In the latter category are the high winds which whip up forest fires in the fall and heavy rains that cause floods and mudslides in winter and spring. Eastern visitors do not expect such excitement in a temperate zone known for its aridity and are quick to criticize the imperfections.

The climate of the Los Angeles basin is, however, generally sunny, warm, and dry. The Pacific Ocean on the west and the mountains to the north and east act as buffers against extremes of summer heat and winter cold. The basin enjoys a Mediterranean-type climate characterized by a dry summer and moderate rainfall in winter—a condition existing on less than three percent of the earth's land surface.

During the summer months, the climate of the basin is influenced by large, slow-moving air masses formed at sea. Those high-pressure anticyclones, which sometimes exceed two thousand miles or more at their widest point, hover along the coast and prevent storms at sea from moving inland. With the approach of winter, however, the coastal air masses begin to drift toward the equator and out to sea and cease to influence storm movements. Between November and March, winter storms, moving from west to east, deposit most of southern California's annual precipitation. Following periods of rainfall, winds frequently shift from the southwest to the north, northwest, or east. That change coaxes continental instead of maritime air into the basin. Dry desert winds, called "Santa Anas," sometimes bring unseasonably warm, midsummer temperatures to the region and divert storms.

PRECIPITATION AT THE LOS ANGELES CIVIC CENTER
1950-1978

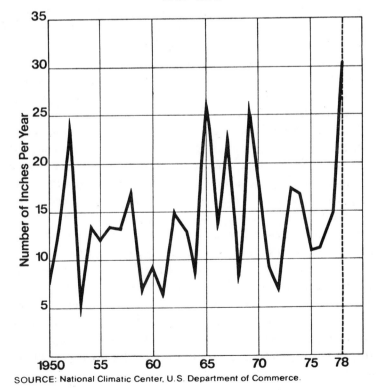

SOURCE: National Climatic Center, U.S. Department of Commerce.

Los Angeles, unlike New York, Buenos Aires, or San Francisco, was not founded at the mouth of a river, yet a river once did flow through its center. The original plaza, laid out in 1791, was located slightly east and north of the present one. In 1818 flooding by the Los Angeles River forced the *pobladores* to move the plaza's location. In 1824 and 1825 the river, indeed, changed its whole stream bed. After leaving today's plaza center, it ran westward along what is today's Washington Boulevard, emptying into La Ballona slough near the present Marina del Rey. After 1825 the river emptied into San Pedro Bay. Before reaching the civic center the Los Angeles River still runs eastward along the mountain range that divides the city from the San Fernando Valley. As a result of this spur in the coastal range, the climate in the valley is generally warmer than that in the older part of the city, which is fanned by prevailing westerly coastal winds and sheltered from the sun (especially in the mornings) by sea fogs.

The city's mild climate attracts tens of thousands of new residents and tourists annually. Mean average temperature in a recent thirty-year period was 63.9 degrees; rarely does the temperature fall below freezing. While the weather pattern includes dry and wet cycles, normal annual rainfall over the same thirty-year period was 14.54 inches. Los Angeles averages 325 days of sunshine a year. Such ideal weather brought the motion picture industry westward, along with manufactures of sportswear and aviation equipment. Despite metropolitan expansion and heavy urbanization, a few farms devoted to fruit growing, market gardening, and livestock still survive in Los Angeles County. A half century ago oranges, lemons, alfalfa, barley, walnuts, sugar beets, celery, lettuce, tomatoes, cauliflower, berries, and flowers were typical local crops.

Without fresh water brought over long distances, the social organism that is Los Angeles and its neighboring cities could not survive. Until 1913 the Los Angeles River and well water were the only sources of supply. Wells still tap the river bed for part of the city's water. Much of the supply now comes from the Los Angeles Aqueduct, a gravity line that extends 238 miles from the Owens River on the eastern slope of the Sierra Nevada. This Owens Valley project has been extended over the years to the back country east of Yosemite National Park. Another aqueduct, completed in 1940 by the Metropolitan Water District of Southern California, carries water some three hundred miles from the Colorado River.

For years Los Angeles boasted a population growth that could only be called phenomenal. During the 1950s nearly 240,000 persons settled in the city each year. This expansion was equaled by few other places. By 1965 the greater metropolitan area had a population of almost 7 million, giving it the character of a city-state. Los Angeles and its satellite cities then claimed more residents than forty-three of the American states. Although population growth tapered off during the 1970s, demographers still believe that before the end of this century an industrial complex, including satellite residential suburbs, will stretch for more than two hundred miles from Santa Barbara to San Diego and reach inland to Palm Springs and San Bernardino.

"Los Angeles," thus, is an umbrella term. The city's cultural and social boundaries extend all the way from Marineland on the Palos Verdes peninsula to the Associated Colleges in Claremont and southeastward toward Disneyland and Palm Springs. The Santa Anita racetrack, Huntington Library, Forest Lawn, the MGM studios, and the *Queen Mary,* docked at Long Beach, form part of these loose confines as does a cluster of universities and colleges. City and county distinctions are blurred by commuters who travel forty and fifty miles from home to work or business.

The expansion of new industries since World War II caused a continuing construction boom in homes and industrial plants on hundreds of new tracts. As the shift from single-family dwellings to apartments and condominiums proceeds, the skyline is changing. With the disappearance of available land, a paved-over city grows increasingly vertical while its rural and horizontal past fades from sight.

The high-rise buildings that jut up into the skyline are symbols of an urbanization that perplexes everyone—even frightens many. The sunshine city of pueblo and rancho days now is polluted with scummy air and water as well as by crime and ethnic conflicts. Traffic jams, increased by the failure to develop mass rapid transit, make commuting ever more difficult. While there are positive advantages to living in Los Angeles, its population sprawl reminds us that this particular society has equated technological expansion with human progress. The explosive growth and prosperity of recent times present Angelenos with unresolved problems. A confusing postindustrial ambience is the result of a failure to fuse humans with the environment in this prototypical city of the future. No amount of self-congratulatory writing, such as characterized the bicentennial year 1981, can obscure the many disrupting future challenges that face the city of Los Angeles.

CHAPTER TWO

The First Inhabitants and Visitors

LONG BEFORE Los Angeles became a remote outpost of the Spanish empire, several Indian villages flourished there. Yang-na, the principal one, consisted of thatch and brush huts. These native communities subsisted by hunting, as well as by the gathering of foodstuffs, and by fishing in nearby streams and at the ocean rather than through sowing or harvesting crops.

There was no ongoing system of agriculture. The epithet "digger"—a term first applied to these and other California natives in contempt of their appearance and diet—is not deserved. The roots for which they did indeed dig formed only part of their food supply. Rabbits and deer meat were everywhere available. A major staple was the acorn, gathered from wild oak trees. Before acorns could be eaten, the natives utilized a complicated process to grind, dry, leach, and sweeten the bitter meal.

Isolated by mountain barriers and deserts, these first inhabitants developed an insular society suited to their needs. Although one may today see them as conservative in outlook, eventually they abandoned their Shoshonean speech and learned Spanish. Some became competent workers under mission tutelage. They had never possessed domesticated animals but became excellent cattle drovers.

The basic Indian communities were called *rancherías* by the Spanish. Eventually these deteriorated as whites chased the natives off their fertile lands onto the rocky deserts and mountains. As a result, the Indian record has largely been obliterated, except for a few place-names like Point Mugu, Pacoima, Malibu, and Cahuenga.

More than two hundred years after Juan Rodríguez Cabrillo began the recorded history of California by landing at San Diego Bay in 1542, a Spanish army captain, Gaspar de Portolá, led a party of explorers and missionaries northward from that harbor to become the first white visitors to the future site of Los Angeles. There, on August 2, 1769, Portolá and his leather-jacketed *soldados* camped. Their campsite was along the banks of a river that he named El Río de Nuestra Señora la Reina de Los Angeles de Porciúncula. Portolá did not, however, found the city of "Our Lady Queen of the Angels." That event would not occur for twelve more years.

Meanwhile, the untamed land still belonged to the local *Indios.* The Gabrielinos, who occupied most of present-day Los Angeles, are today extinct. They lived in semipermanent village communities. In 1769 they met the Portolá party with baskets of seeds and shell beads while the Spaniards gave the natives tobacco and glass beads in return. These Indians could hardly suspect that they would become an important part of a future work force.[1]

Father Juan Crespi of Portolá's party was among the first to look upon the Los Angeles countryside, noting particularly the many wild rose bushes in full bloom and the river. His superior, Father Junípero Serra, was to become founder of Alta California's chain of missions. On September 8, 1771, Serra founded Mission San Gabriel Arcángel, a few miles east of the future city. Its museum, displaying clerical relics, occupies the former living quarters of the padres. Similarly, the San Fernando Mission Historical Museum consists of original and restored buildings and includes early artifacts. U.S. Highway 101 follows the old "King's Highway" of the tourist literature (El Camino Real) northward from San Diego, linking these missions. Fifty-eight miles south of Los Angeles is Mission San Juan Capistrano. The plaza church, within Los Angeles proper, was built much later.

The explorer Juan Bautista de Anza, who opened up the overland route from Mexico to California in 1774, also had an influence on the future city. Anza, like Portolá, was a military trailbreaker. He saw that the opening of a route northwestward from the Mexican province of Sonora to the Pacific would provide an alternative to the long and perilous sea voyage on which California still relied for contact with the outside world. The shorter route, he believed, would make it easier to transport needed settlers and provisions to the remote provinces. His recommendations were accepted by Spain's viceroy at Mexico City, Antonio María Bucareli, who ordered him in January 1774 to lead a band of thirty-four men through the sand and sagebrush, with Father Francisco Garcés as his guide, from Tubac in northern Mexico to California. On March 22, 1774, Anza's party was enthusiastically greeted by the padres at Mission San Gabriel. He had opened the first overland route to southern California, a bleak, long, but practical trail. The formal founding of Los Angeles followed, even though Indian attacks would intermittently close Anza's route.

On the eastern seaboard of North America, meanwhile, the American war of independence was concluding. Spain had retaken Florida from the British and aided American troops in the Ohio Valley. In the fall of 1781, just six weeks before the British surrendered to George Washington at Yorktown, Felipe de Neve, governor of Spanish California, founded the pueblo of Los Angeles. His first *pobladores* consisted of eleven couples with twenty-two children. These forty-four persons were mostly mestizos, blacks, Indians, and mulattoes with an admixture of Spanish blood. Among the original settlers was Antonio María Lugo, a six-year-old lad who would become one of the most affluent *rancheros* in California. The first inhabitants included a handful of earthy peasants, a cowherder, a tailor, and a mason.[2] These were escorted by a detachment of seventeen soldiers garbed in blue jackets with yellow buttons. Some had walked overland from Álamos in Sonora, south of the present Mexican border, while others had come via Baja California.

After Governor De Neve personally read the provisions of Spanish law for the establishment of a pueblo, he held a modest parade and his men fired a lone cannon. De Neve then left

Corporal José Vicente Féliz in charge as "little father of the pueblo."

The development of better overland routes from northern Mexico increased the number of settlers. The colonists cleared the wild mustard and sagebrush and took up land granted them by Spain's authority. They thereby began the great southern California ranchos of the future, some of which were to be larger than whole European countries.

Yet it was difficult to induce colonials of standing to accept a form of exile to such a distant wilderness. Instead, humble people laid out the pueblo's first plaza, or birthplace. In 1786, five years after its founding, the first land titles were officially issued to the pueblo's residents. Each recipient affixed his cross to the documents. Not one of them could write his name.

The founding of Los Angeles, albeit delayed, had resulted from Spain's determination to tighten control over California. England, France, and Russia had shown an interest in the Pacific Coast. In spite of Spain's efforts to keep foreigners out, visitors from abroad spread the word about the isolated province. In 1803, the *Lelia Byrd* became the first United States vessel officially to touch at San Pedro, the port of Los Angeles. The glowing account of trading possibilities in California that her master carried back to New England brought other Americans to the West Coast. Some sailors stayed on, occasionally marrying Spanish women and adopting the Catholic faith. Cattle-raising on the ranchos formed the predominant pattern during this pastoral age. Gradually the countryside resembled a patchwork of ranchos settled by former soldiers, government officials, and foreigners.

In 1784 Spain had awarded the first permit to graze cattle to three families—the Verdugos, Nietos, and Domínguezes. Later Corporal José Vicente Féliz was granted Rancho Los Féliz, and Miguel Ortega received the grant called Las Vírgenes. Most of California's approximately eight hundred land grants were awarded later during the Mexican period. There was to be much confusion over hazy boundaries created by the haphazard methods of geographical description employed by a succession of poorly trained granting officials.

Community life at Los Angeles revolved around its plaza. Facing on it were a council house, storeroom, and jail; the remaining frontage was occupied by dwellings. By 1784 the colonists had replaced their first rude huts with better adobe homes, and they laid the foundations for a church and other public buildings. In time it would become the height of fashion for the Carrillos, Olveras, and Sepúlvedas to build handsome "plaza front" town houses. (Near today's Southwest Museum, several miles to the north, is the Casa de Adobe, a replica of such adobes from about the year 1800.) On Sundays people crowded the square to hear mass, to sing, to watch bull and cock fights, and to play *monte.*

According to the census of 1790 the population of "El Pueblo," as it came to be called, had increased to 139. This growth was due, in part, to the arrival from the Santa Barbara and San Diego presidios of retired *soldados* who became civilian residents. They were joined in 1818 by the pueblo's first *yanqui,* Joseph Chapman, a Bostonian, who mistakenly came to be called "El Ingles," or the Englishman. He had deserted the pseudorevolutionary Hippolyte de Bouchard's piratical coastal raiding party. Chapman quickly left behind his life as a pirate, becoming a skilled carpenter and jack-of-all-trades. He helped build the new plaza church during the year of his arrival.

Today's Plaza (bounded by Main, Los Angeles, and Plaza streets and Sunset Boulevard) is not on the site of the original one. The sculptured figure of Father Junípero Serra looks across another square than that abandoned in 1818 after a flood. Around this new plaza is a church rebuilt on higher ground, as well as Olvera Street, and the reconstructed Ávila Adobe. Lugo House, until it was torn down in 1949, was the oldest two-story building in Los Angeles; it was built in 1850 by Vicente Lugo. Nearby stands the three-story Pico House, constructed in 1869 by Pío Pico, last of California's Mexican governors. With its gaslights, indoor water closets, and caged birds in the courtyard, this was the best hotel in the city for several decades and the first three-story building. Now partially restored, it is a tourist center, with shops and restaurants handily nearby.

Olvera Street carries the name of Agustín Olvera, an early official. It is now lined by shops, booths, and restaurants, having been first restored in the 1930s. La Zanja Madre (mother ditch) Fountain, opposite 35 Olvera Street, is a remnant of the open ditch which once supplied water from the Los Angeles River.

Vicente Lugo ranch house and some of its landlords and neighbors, 1892.
(*C. C. Pierce Collection; by courtesy of the Huntington Library, San Marino, California.*)

Large wooden water wheels lifted the water from the *zanjas,* or ditches, leading into the plaza area. Because the square wooden piping used for conduits has long since disappeared, there is only one remnant of this water supply system left behind for today's tourists to view.

The political instability in Mexico was reflected in Los Angeles. After 1821, following a revolutionary struggle against Spain, a succession of regimes, under a new and weak Mexican government, hampered the social and economic stability of the sleepy little town. Yet it only vicariously experienced the rumblings of this turmoil to the south. Distance and the difficulty of communication with Mexico, plus strong local pride, encouraged an attitude of separateness in California. One measure of this was the increasing use of the term *Californio* to identify a local resident.

Another result of the break with Spain was the dispersal of lands formerly belonging to the missions. This process was known as "secularization." In the early 1830s the California governors were ordered by the Mexican congress to give each head of a family within the California pueblos a *solar* of land not to exceed 400 *varas* (a *vara* was equal to 33 inches) square. This came out of the common lands of the missions. In the case of Los Angeles the nearest missions were San Fernando and San Gabriel. Settlements—some containing less than twenty-five families—developed on these lands at the edge of the pueblo and could be considered suburbs. This process speeded up the decentralization of Los Angeles. The authority of local officials was also diffused as a result of the secularization edicts, which tok many years to implement, so inefficient was the bureaucracy of Mexico's faraway colony.

In today's urban complex it is difficult to imagine the rural environment, in which pueblo, mission, and rancho interacted. For most of its history Los Angeles was a farming community. The townsfolk mingled with the *rancheros* in the surrounding countryside with few barriers erected. Cattle roamed over great unfenced tracts and irrigation rights were enjoyed by *rancheros, pobladores,* and *Indios* alike.

Partly because of California's political instability, intruding foreigners also came to play an important role in local affairs. After 1822 New England shipmasters and merchants began to appear along the southern California coastline. They were in search of hides and tallow which they paid for with such manu- factured products as needles, boots, and shoes. Most of these pre-pioneer foreigners did not return to the province. But a few settled, principally at Monterey or Yerba Buena (later San Fran- cisco). The agents of shipping companies, called "supercargoes," were in a position to enrich themselves rather quickly because of the scarcity of the luxuries which they offered as barter. Other merchants came overland with supplies and eastern con- tracts that also proved valuable.

One of these traders who ended up staying at Los Angeles was Abel Stearns, later affectionately known as "Cara de Ca- ballo," or Horseface. Revised mercantile regulations allowed him to exchange goods for local products. By importing silks, hardward, boots, and other indispensable "finished goods," Don Abel and the trader John Temple delivered vital supplies to isolated, pre-American Los Angeles.

Stearns was, in the words of historian Robert Glass Cleland, "the personification of an age." His life pattern, therefore, merits special attention. Even before gold was discovered at Sutter's Fort in 1848, Stearns purchased and shipped as much as a million dollars worth of that metal to the Philadelphia mint. He obtained his gold from the San Francisquito Canyon and other local placers. Don Abel, as he came to be called, was interested in more than merchandising. With Thomas Oliver Larkin, American consul at California's capital of Monterey, he worked toward a peaceful annexation of the province to the United States, which did not occur. The Stearns home, known as El Palacio de Don Abel, was located on the southeast corner of Arcadia and Main streets. To this spacious one-story adobe, he, at age forty-three, took his teen-aged bride, Arcadia Bandini. (Her unmarried sisters were also to live with them.) With his beautiful wife as hostess, Stearns made El Palacio both a social and a political center of southern California life. By 1860 he owned over 200,000 acres and had become the wealthiest and most influential landowner and merchant south of San Francisco. Long before Stearns died in 1871, he gave his wife the Laguna Rancho, consisting of 11,000 acres in the very center of Los Angeles. Despite serious losses from several droughts and legal complications, Doña Arcadia became a wealthy widow twice, for she also married another man of great means, Robert S. Baker.

The way in which parts of the Stearns ranchos were ultimately subdivided set the pattern for later extensive real-estate developments. Temple and Baker, too, became more than prominent local citizens. Backed up, of course, by the Hispanic heritage of their wives, eventually they came to be relied upon as virtual sustainers of the Los Angeles scene. These *yanquis,* harbingers of the dominant culture, not only married into the local families of prominence; some also took up the Catholic faith and became adopted *hijos del país,* or sons of the country. The legacy of these early years would, indeed, pass more and more into the hands of invading Americans. The land which sold at eighty cents per acre in 1857 increased to $50 per acre in 1900 and to $700 per acre in 1912, the year when Doña Arcadia Bandini Stearns Baker died.[3]

Cattle, sheep, and horses once far outnumbered people in

Los Angeles County. The cattle frontier has disappeared. Sheep no longer graze on the coastal plains. Horses, now rented by the half hour at rundown stables, must be ridden along prescribed trails, away from the traffic that clogs the highways. Stage coaches gave way first to railroads, then to trucks and airplanes. Even the working ranch houses of the past are hard to find. Today, hidden away and secluded near Long Beach, are a few acres surrounding two adobes that mark ranchos which numbered thousands of acres. This was once the site of Los Cerritos and of the Los Alamitos spreads. The Temple, Stearns, and Bixby families owned these lands. Los Cerritos alone numbered 26,000 acres. The children of these families could ride horseback along miles of shoreline which formed their private beaches.

That was a slower-paced world than ours. Quiet and serenity reigned. Engulfed by mechanization, it has long since disappeared, except perhaps in mind. Southern California's Arcadian era is also partially recoverable through manuscripts, account books, and such material objects as branding irons and crumbling adobe fragments. But the cattle no longer roam the thousand hills of a receding past.

CHAPTER THREE

El Pueblo
and the
Yankees

L OS ANGELES participated in the gradual shift from Mexican to United States rule as Americans came into the town from the sea and overland. The sleepy pueblo might have remained dormant for many years if these Yankees had not crossed the seemingly impenetrable wilderness of desert and mountains to the east.

In 1826, Jedediah Strong Smith, a young trapper of New England parentage, blazed a trail from the Missouri frontier settlements to southern California. At the head of a small group of fur hunters, Smith sought beaver, but his trek southwestward had a larger significance and has kindled the imagination of historians. At the age of twenty-eight, he became the first white man to reach California by an overland route from the eastern United States. After traveling through hundreds of miles of wilderness and undergoing Indian attacks as well as severe shortages of food and water, he and his bedraggled group finally reached Mission San Gabriel. Their arrival astonished its mission priests, who received the strangers warmly, but California's suspicious governor, José María Echeandía, ordered Smith's party to leave the territory. Only recently did historians learn that he had also visited the pueblo of Los Angeles.[1]

More important for Smith, Governor Echeandía imprisoned him in a dirty San Diego jail and freed him only after he promised never to return to California. If such intrusions by foreign interlopers went unchecked, other trapping parties might well enter the province. And Smith *was* followed by other American trappers, adventurers whose trails helped to open up southern California.

One of these trappers, James Ohio Pattie, provided an excellent description of Los Angeles in 1828:

> The houses have flat roofs, covered with bituminous pitch, brought from a place within four miles of the town, where this article boils up from the earth. As the liquid rises, hollow bubbles, like a shell of large size, are formed. When they burst, the noise is heard distinctly in the town.[2]

Pattie, like Smith, had been arrested by Governor Echeandía, but was freed because he promised to travel throughout the province and to vaccinate the population against smallpox. At Los Angeles he reportedly vaccinated 2,500 persons, probably an exaggerated figure.

Another trader who visited southern California was William Wolfskill, a Kentuckian who first arrived in Los Angeles in 1831 by way of the Cajon Pass and San Bernardino. He pioneered the pack-train route later known as the Old Spanish Trail and became a settler.[3]

In 1820 the pueblo's population was only 650, while Monterey then had 700 inhabitants, of which 100 were troops from its presidio. By the mid-1830s Los Angeles became the larger community, numbering about a thousand residents in addition to several hundred Indians who labored for them. In 1835 the Mexican congress declared Los Angeles the capital of the Californias, north and south. But this edict, which promoted it to the rank of *ciudad,* was not enforced by those governors who favored Monterey in the north. So the city was still referred to as "el pueblo." Ten years later, however, and only for a short time, Governor Pío Pico, California's last Mexican chief executive, removed the capital to Los Angeles. He established his headquarters in an adobe building later to become the Bella Union hotel. North-south factional struggles seemed to be at their height at the very time when a greater dispute between Mexico and the United States reached a climax.

By then Mexico's governors seemed helpless to stop arriving Americans. Growing in numbers yearly, and especially in their influence, they were a determined, energetic lot. Once they began to show up in overland parties, their presence added a new element to the population. Among the early pioneer groups to appear at Los Angeles was the Workman-Rowland party. Largely from Missouri frontier towns, the members of this party were in search of new homes. Driving along sheep as sustenance, they arrived in Los Angeles in 1841 by way of the Santa Fe Trail, Cajon Pass, and Mission San Gabriel. Their leader, John Rowland, received a welcome of sorts, notwithstanding a previous warning by the Mexican authorities against mass American immigration into the province. Among these newcomers was Benjamin D. Wilson, one of the founders of Pasadena, after whom Mount Wilson was later named. (He was also the grandfather of General George Patton.)

Few of the pueblo's residents could possibly have imagined how great were the changes that lay ahead. For nearly a decade Mexico and the United States had been unable to resolve a serious dispute over Texas. When James K. Polk came to the American presidency, it was clear that Mexico was too weak to protect California against foreign challenges. Their very debility made the Mexicans especially outraged by the United States Navy's premature raising of the American flag at Monterey in 1842 and by the arrival of the flamboyant explorer-naturalist John Charles Frémont early in 1846. The Bear Flag Revolt further upset the province's Mexican authorities.

Soon after the Mexican War broke out, American naval forces entered Los Angeles and, during the afternoon of August 13, 1846, Commodore Robert F. Stockton quickly concluded what may be called "the first conquest of California." He left Marine Captain Archibald Gillespie in command of the city with a garrison of fifty men. Soon Gillespie was beleaguered on a hill at the center of the pueblo by Sérvulo Varelas and a group of resentful *pobladores* who assaulted his tiny garrison on September 23. These locals were incensed by restrictions placed upon their movements within and without the city by the tactless young American placed in charge of their lives. Eventually six hundred indignant citizens completely surrounded his forces.[4]

Gillespie sent a courier northward under cover of darkness for aid from Commodore Stockton. The almost legendary horseback ride of Juan Flaco, or "Lean John"—the Paul Revere of California history—covered the distance between Los Angeles and San Francisco in about four and a half days. The appeal for help which he delivered to Stockton was written on cigarette papers and concealed in his long hair.

Meanwhile, the partisans (now commanded by José María Flores) who had besieged Gillespie allowed the hated American to retreat under a flag of truce to San Pedro. Gillespie had to agree, however, that his force would depart by sea from that port. The women of Los Angeles, to show their covert hostility, presented the young Marine officer with a basket of peaches rolled in cactus spines. Gillespie apparently went back on his word when 350 men sent by Stockton to relieve him appeared at San Pedro. He had, of course, made the hasty agreement to retreat under duress and in a state of siege. The Americans, however, still faced some fifty horsemen under José Antonio Carrillo. The skirmish in which they became engaged came to be known as the Battle of the Old Woman's Gun. The Angelenos were mounted on horses and armed with sharp willow lances and carbines; their most damaging weapon, however, was a four-pound brass field piece. An antique firearm, it had been hidden by an old woman during the first American assault on Los Angeles. Dragged about by leather *reatas* attached to the saddles of the attacking partisans, this miniature cannon forced Gillespie's men to retreat to their ships.

Anti-American opposition spread, and the territory from Santa Barbara to San Diego again momentarily fell into the hands of the Californians. Stockton now joined General Stephen Watts Kearny, marching westward from Santa Fe. Kearny had run into unexpected opposition further south from more than 150 Californians under Andrés Pico at the Battle of San Pascual (near present-day Escondido). Together they left San Diego on December 29 to reattack Los Angeles. At the same time, John Charles Frémont approached the city from the north with his force.[5]

Kearny and Stockton, in their march on Los Angeles, met no real opposition until they reached the banks of the San Gabriel River near the present city of Montebello. They fought the final conflict of the Mexican War in California. Known as the Battle of La Mesa, it permitted reoccupation of Los Angeles. On January 10, 1847, American troops entered "the City of the Angels" and marched to its plaza, where Lieutenant Gillespie once more hoisted the flag he had been ignominiously compelled to haul down the previous September. Stockton treated villagers assembled at the plaza to a band concert which helped smooth over past hard feelings.

It was Frémont, however, who received the surrender of the last armed forces in California. On January 13, 1847, two days after Frémont entered the San Fernando Valley with a battalion of 400 mounted riflemen, Andrés Pico surrendered to him on the outskirts of Los Angeles; they signed a truce known as the Cahuenga Capitulation. In July, American forces at Los Angeles were joined by a volunteer Mormon battalion under Lieutenant Colonel Philip St. George Cook. On the hill where Gillespie had been besieged, the reinforced invaders built a fort with timbers from the nearby San Gabriel Mountains. They named the site Fort Moore Hill after one of their dead.[6] In 1848, with the war between the United States and Mexico ended, the peace treaty gave the United States its vast Southwest, of which Los Angeles eventually became the hub.

Today one can visit the Campo de Cahuenga in North Hollywood, where Frémont and Pico signed the peace treaty that terminated hostilities between the Californians and U.S. forces. Some miles away, overlooking the Los Angeles Civic Center, is the Fort Moore Pioneer Memorial, which consists of an artificial waterfall and a series of decorative friezes.

After a short period under military rule, Los Angeles reverted to civilian control and "El Pueblo" officially became Americanized. Soon agitation grew for a civilian state government. In 1849, representatives of the new city went to the state's first constitutional convention at Monterey. Although Los Angeles never became the capital of American California, it grew steadily more important economically. On April 4, 1850, the city was designated as the county seat. That year the first English-language school was opened and the first Protestant church established.

Los Angeles in 1850. (*Courtesy of Copley Books, San Diego, California.*)

A mayor replaced the *alcalde,* and the *ayuntamiento* gave way to a city council. The Hispanic past had come to an end, but only as to law. A United States government report of November 1849 provides a revealing description of how the city looked then:

> From the San Gabriel it is about eight miles further to the town of Los Angeles, where about four miles up and down the stream the river bottom is covered with vineyards, orchards, and gardens, through which wind lanes leading to town. . . . [The town is] close under the hills on the north side of the valley, and consists of an old adobe church, and about a hundred adobe houses scattered around a dusty plaza, and along three or four broad streets leading thereto.[7]

In 1850, some sixty-nine years after the town's settlers had camped along the banks of the Porciúncula, the first United States census showed that the city had a population of only 1,610. The passage of years had not meant the end of the frontier era. That same federal census showed only 7,017 females and 85,580 males throughout the state (making a total California population of but 92,597 inhabitants). Still, this number of residents allowed California, a prize of war, that year to join the American union as the thirty-first state.

In 1850 Los Angeles was again officially proclaimed a city, this time by its new American rulers. They gave its surrounding county the same name. The Los Angeles hinterland encompassed an area almost as large as the state of Ohio, including all of today's Orange and San Bernardino counties as well as part of Kern and Riverside counties. The huge land mass that had become Los Angeles can be seen as one of the results of that materialistic enterprise which had not existed when the first Yankees began to displace the Latino heritage. El Pueblo had given way to the crushing force of an Anglo-American future whose ultimate shape no one could yet foretell.

CHAPTER FOUR

Gold and Commerce

F EW PERSONS TODAY realize that gold was first discovered near Los Angeles a half-dozen years before the great gold strike of 1848 in northern California. Indeed, even in Spanish colonial times the mission padres cautioned the natives not to divulge the location of gold, lest the province be inundated by foreigners.

The secret of California's hidden treasure was eventually bound to be revealed. In 1842 a *ranchero* named Francisco López went to San Feliciano Canyon (eight miles from modern Newhall) in search of stray horses. While stopping to rest, he used a "sheaf knife" to dig up wild onions on whose roots he noticed some bright flakes. Hearing of López's find, several hundred men uncovered enough gold in the same canyon to send a sizable quantity to the government mint at Philadelphia. If the San Feliciano lode had not been so shallow, Los Angeles— instead of San Francisco and Sacramento—might have become the focus of the California gold rush in 1848.

One effect of the much larger discovery of gold in the Sierra Nevada was the demand for beef and other supplies. Miners looked to Los Angeles for sustenance and the town became known as "Queen of the Cow Counties." Its large nearby ranchos, their hills dense with cattle, prospered for a time. *Rancheros* used their new wealth to build larger adobe homes, furnished

with expensive furniture and fancy clothes. But they also encountered costly lawsuits necessary to defend their land titles
against avaricious American squatters who had crossed the
plains in search of vacant land.

In 1849, because of the uncertainty of its early land titles,
Lieutenant E. O. C. Ord of the United States Army officially
mapped the Los Angeles pueblo. This enabled residents to sell
lots with greater security, although only in 1866 did President
Andrew Johnson confirm the city's 17,000 acres of pueblo land
titles. This action was particularly important, for the claims of
numerous grants issued by the original pueblo rested on these
titles. Ord's map designated streets with both English and Spanish names; Calle Principal became Main Street and Calle Prima-
vera, Spring Street.

As the flush days brought by the gold rush faded, the demand
for local beef lessened. Indebted *rancheros* had overspent themselves on luxury goods during years of prosperity, and they were
still attempting to prove to the courts that they owned the
ranchos where they had lived for so many years. These lawsuits
continued to drain away their wealth. It took many years to
straighten out overlapping land claims under two systems of law.

In the years before the Civil War, San Francisco, not Los
Angeles, became the most powerful and cosmopolitan city west
of St. Louis. For a decade and a half after banks were in
existence at San Francisco there was none at Los Angeles; Isaias
W. Hellman's first city bank opened only in 1865. Relatively
few theatrical and literary figures were attracted to Los Angeles
in these years. The southern counties, with but a small population, remained primarily agricultural. Friction early developed
between the areas. The southerners felt that state taxes levied
upon their cattle and land were disproportionate to those col-
lected in the northern mining area. Indeed, this sectional feeling
grew so strong that in 1859 a proposal to divide the state was
sent by local partisans to President James Buchanan. Primarily
because of the later American Civil War, nothing came of the
plan. Today the populous areas are in the south, the "cow
counties" in the north. While there are continuing suggestions
to split California into two parts, few take them seriously.

Eventually the economic development of Los Angeles came

to be closely related to the growth of transportation. Primitive mule and pack-train service gave way to stages which ran twice a month between San Francisco and Los Angeles. So poor was mail delivery that for six weeks during the harsh winter of 1852–1853, Los Angeles received no regular mail. In 1857 Congress finally voted an overland mail bill and John Butterfield, successful bidder for the franchise, started his cross-country stages moving toward Los Angeles in September of the following year.[1] Waterman L. Ormsby, a New York newspaper correspondent who arrived on this first stage on October 7, 1858, observed that the town contained some fine buildings and about six thousand residents. Ormsby was more impressed, however, with the local vineyards and orchards than by the inhabitants.

Here and there properties still exist that reflect the rancho style of life which merged into the American ambience. The Los Angeles State and County Arboretum, a 127-acre park, is situated on land once owned by Elias Jackson Baldwin, known as "Lucky" Baldwin. He came to California in 1853 and had become a millionaire by the 1870s. His Queen Anne cottage, built near the adobe of Hugo Reid, has, like that earlier building, been restored and is open to visitors.[2] Nearby, in the area that came to be called Rosemead, L. J. Rose developed a similar property named Sunny Slope.

A picturesque episode in the story of southwestern transportation began with the authorization by Congress of a "Camel Corps." On the eighth of January, 1858, after the first of these animals had made their way westward from Arizona (swimming the Colorado River en route), the population turned out to witness their entrance into Los Angeles. These caravans were a short-lived experiment, designed to test the adaptability of camels to the western scene. The camels were eventually let loose on the desert where, for some years thereafter, they were occasionally spotted by bemused travelers.

The development of transportation in Los Angeles is linked with the name of Phineas Banning, who arrived from Delaware in 1851. Unlike other contemporaries, he did not go on to the northern goldfields but settled at San Pedro, which he helped develop into a safe port. He also imported Abbott and Downing

136059

coaches from Concord, New Hampshire. In 1854, with Benjamin D. Wilson, John Downey, and William Sanford, he
bought 2,400 acres of Rancho San Pedro from Manuel Domín-
guez. They paid one dollar per acre, and transformed what came
to be called "Banning's Goose Pond" at "New San Pedro" into a
promising ship landing. Remembering his native Delaware, he
renamed the place Wilmington. Known eventually as the father
of Los Angeles harbor, Banning was also involved in overland
freight and passenger communications by both stage and rail. In
addition to this, he owned coastal steamers. In 1867 Banning
began to operate a regular stage service between the ocean and
Los Angeles. Cushioned against the buffetings of roads full of
holes, his leather-cradled thoroughbrace carriages were greatly
preferable to fixed-axle wagons.[4]

Early stage drivers ran the risk of encountering outlaws along
routes of travel into Los Angeles. One such bandit, Joaquín
Murieta, was particularly notorious. In the 1850s another high-
wayman who infested the area was Juan Flores, expert with his
pistol and "uncannily clever with the knife." He was a quasi-
revolutionary opposed to Anglo domination. He was hanged
for his views and banditry. A third bandit was Tiburcio Vásquez,
captured in 1874 only after he had evaded the law for years.
Vásquez and Murieta became virtual folk heroes with considerable Latino support. After Vásquez and his gang were captured
by a posse, throngs of malcontents visited him in jail. He had
been wounded six times while trying to escape from Alessandro
Repetto's ranch outside Los Angeles, where he had captured
Repetto and demanded a ransom. Before Vásquez was hanged
he had hoped to make a speech on revolution at the scaffold.[5]

From the 1850s onward Los Angeles garnered a reputation as
one of the half-wild cities of the West. Yet it was not as unsavory
as Tombstone or Deadwood. Nevertheless, in an atmosphere of
drinking, gambling, and carousing, Los Angeles experienced
each week at least one death by shooting or knifing. Gunfire and
drunken Indians on Main Street contrasted with the previous
quietude of the adobes along La Calle Principal. Prostitutes and
outlaws, driven out of San Francisco by its active vigilance com-
mittees, moved south into an area of Los Angeles called "Sonora
town." Lynchings and racial tension over Mexicans made Los
Angeles a rallying place for bandits. The files of the *Los Angeles*

Star, southern California's first substantial newspaper, are re-
plete with stories of almost daily violence during the 1860s.

A particularly notorious locale was the Calle de los Negros,
then known as "Nigger Alley." On October 23, 1871, almost
two dozen Chinese were murdered near that street in a dis-
graceful racial pogrom. Several hundred of these "Celestials"
had moved south after the gold rush ended and the railroad
lines had been completed. They became local merchants, operated a laundry or two, dug ditches, and were employed as
domestics. Conflict between rival business tongs had touched
off an incident in which a policeman was shot and a rancher
killed in the crossfire. Because of these casualties, a white mob
took its vengeance. Looting and lynching ensued. The episode,
one of the bloodiest in the history of California, was ignored by
the law, surely because those who were massacred were of
another race.

While Los Angeles at times resembled a lawless frontier
town, there was a discernible yearning for a better society.
Below the surface of crude street violence, a public conscience
stirred, waiting to be awakened and charged with building a real
city, not just a cowtown.

CHAPTER FIVE

From War to Depression and Boom

T HE 1860 CENSUS listed some four thousand residents in Los Angeles. Henry Mellus, its mayor, was a New Englander who had first come to California on the *Pilgrim* with Richard Henry Dana. There were also many southerners. That year Angelenos voted overwhelmingly for the Democratic Party, particularly for its "Chivalry," or secessionist branch. The editor of the *Los Angeles Star,* Henry Hamilton, scarcely disguised his admiration for what came to be called "the peculiar institution" of slavery. Other local advocates of a Confederate victory over Union forces during the Civil War were vocal and active. On occasion residents from the border states of Kentucky, Tennessee, and Missouri unfurled Confederate flags.

After the firing on Fort Sumter, the *Star* regularly attacked Abraham Lincoln and his administration. The paper was banned from the mails and Hamilton was locked up. Friends interceded on his behalf, and when he was released hundreds of his readers rejoiced; later Hamilton was elected to the state senate. After Confederate forces led an attack on New Mexico and Arizona, there was fear that pro-southerners might gain a foothold in southern California. But the area remained loyal to the Union cause. During 1862–1863, incidentally, the Army Camel Corps carried freight via Los Angeles between Fort Tejon and the Drum Barracks at Wilmington (the only major Civil War monument in California).[1]

Far more damaging to the existing society of southern California than the war was a series of fateful events that occurred during the early 1860s. Now the "squatter problem" really began to aggravate life on the ranchos. From the late 1850s onward, depressed cattle prices, as well as severe droughts and heavy intermittent rains, further weakened social stability. *Rancheros* who had borrowed money at ruinous interest rates lost their lands to American creditors. One could speak of these years as those when the *ranchero's* way of life slid into decay. Large cattle ranchos surrounding Los Angeles were subdivided into small plots on which new settlers turned to raising corn and barley as well as hay. These newcomers sometimes usurped land that was not legally theirs.

Only a few *rancheros* knew how to adapt to the invading *yanqui* pattern. By 1861 the price of cattle had fallen so low that many *rurales* moved into the city's center. The little village began to extend itself north and east as water wells supplanted the old *zanja* or open ditch system, with the water stored at the plaza center within a new brick reservoir.

The development of America's first transcontinental rail system was to further even more the physical growth of Los Angeles. In 1865, while still building its transcontinental system, the Central Pacific Railroad Company chartered the Southern Pacific Railroad and incorporated smaller branch lines. Los Angeles, eager for an outlet to market its products, wanted a tie-in with this network, but enticement of the railroad required money. The Southern Pacific system was accused of extorting funds from towns along prospective routes. The railroad, claiming to need money with which to build bridges and overpasses, as well as for the grading of track beds, forced Los Angeles to produce a subsidy of more than $600,000, to provide land for a depot, and to surrender control of an existing twenty-two-mile rail line to Wilmington. The sharp-eyed Phineas Banning had in 1869 built this line, called the Los Angeles and San Pedro Railway. Indeed, he had unloaded at his Wilmington dock the first locomotive to be used locally, offering a free excursion trip into Los

Angeles that year. The completion of this link between city and sea had stimulated the growth of Los Angeles from about six thousand persons in 1870 to eleven thousand by 1880.

The Southern Pacific operations, however, would dwarf all previous local transportation achievements. On September 5, 1876, that railroad held a ceremony at Lang's Station in Soledad Pass to mark the opening of a rail link between Los Angeles and San Francisco over the Tehachapis. Charles Crocker, president of the Southern Pacific, hammered a gold spike into the final tie. That evening there was more celebrating in Los Angeles, where residents hoped that this new link with the East would expand the market for local agricultural products.

In 1881 Los Angeles held its centennial celebration. Some thirty thousand spectators attended a circus, watched fireworks, and heard speeches in three languages. The "city" itself had a population of only 11,183 inhabitants. The grand marshal was George Stoneman, who had arrived in 1847 with the Mormon Battalion. He was to become governor of California in 1883.

By 1885 the Santa Fe Railroad reached Los Angeles. Its entry gave the city another eastern rail connection, and this broke the monopoly of the Southern Pacific. The competition touched off a rate war with the SP that resulted in a flood of population. In 1887, at the height of the rivalry, passenger fares from the Midwest dropped from $125 to as little as one dollar. These rates encouraged unprecedented transcontinental travel. In the decade of the 1880s alone Los Angeles grew from a pueblo with dirt streets into a bustling, paved city of 50,395. Perhaps as many as two hundred thousand persons came through the area during that boom period.

Among the new residents who sought to exchange harsh winters for year-round sunshine were unemployed ranch hands, fruit pickers, dispossessed midwestern wheat farmers, engineers, health seekers, and real-estate promoters. Tradesmen, artisans, and merchants became their own best customers and created a prosperity that fed upon itself.

Technology quickly spread. Telephones and electric lights were installed in 1882. Four years later street cars appeared. Drawn at first by horses, then fueled by electric cables, they left the city center at Spring and Second streets and moved beyond fashionable Bunker Hill toward the periphery of Los Angeles.

Broadway, looking south from Second Street in Los Angeles, 1889. On June 8 of that year the cable car route opened. (*C. C. Pierce Collection; by courtesy of the Huntington Library, San Marino, California.*)

The first interurban streetcar system, constructed by "General" Moses Sherman, began operation during 1895. Its cars, propelled by electricity, operated between the central city and Pasadena. Later Henry E. Huntington (nephew of the better known Southern Pacific mogul, Collis P.) expanded that system and formed his Pacific Electric Railway Company out of seventy-three existing local lines. After the turn of the century, his "Big Red Cars" covered an area sixty miles in width and transported people to the beaches, the mountains, and the agricultural areas as well as to his new real-estate subdivisions.

Although the city hailed new technology, it also welcomed with the same enthusiasm older ideas. The gathering of so many midwestern Protestants, for example, made the place a bastion for temperance advocates. The Women's Christian Temperance Union (WCTU), which wished to ban the serving of alcoholic beverages, railed against the state's wine industry. The regulation of barrooms was peculiarly effective at Los Angeles, where there were sixty-two saloons by 1872. Saloonkeepers could be fined $50 for staying open on Sundays. Yet saloons continued to prosper and fared better than churches—just as today's sports fans far outnumber the members of historical societies or ladies' clubs.

Within less than two years after 1887, various land syndicate groups "platted" a hundred communities with five hundred thousand lots on large tracts of waterless land inside the borders of Los Angeles County. (Two years later Orange County was carved out of its hinterland.) Buying cheap arid real estate, these developers began to form large family fortunes. Los Angeles—though lacking in coal, lumber, and metals, isolated on the far side of North America, and still without a fully developed harbor—had embarked on a period of prodigious growth. This was spurred by extravagant realty advertising, the lure of a mild climate, and fierce railroad competition.

The land-boom advertising, abetted by the railroads, skillfully exploited the similarities between southern California and the ancient world. Local olives, citrus, and craggy cliffs did indeed remind persons familiar with Italy of the bay of Naples. The comparison, which stressed both ancient world and romantic future, was carried over enthusiastically into the naming of new "instant towns": Hesperia, Rialto, Tarragona, Terracina, Verona. At one such namesake, Venice, developers featured imitation lagoons and terraced piazzas.

The bustling Mediterranea that surrounded Los Angeles was ripe for swindlers, unscrupulous real-estate agents, and loan sharks. The selling of lots and acreage took place on the streets, in bars, and in restaurants. To draw crowds, developers utilized elephants, brass bands, and free lunches. Former rancho land, described as residential property but located in the middle of stream beds, was sold to unsuspecting newcomers.[2]

All this growth surprised even the shrewdest promoters, for most of the cities and towns born during the boom of the 1880s survived. Indeed, these communities not only prospered—their residents lived to see later booms and larger migrations. In 1888 businessmen organized a chamber of commerce to lure eastern residents during periods of lesser population influx. Construc-

The interior of the Bradbury Building, constructed in 1893. (*Courtesy Security Pacific National Bank.*)

tion within central Los Angeles was featured on its colored posters. New edifices included the Bradbury Building (1893), an impressive structure that took advantage of southern California sunshine in ways that still delight visitors.

Experimentation with rail transport was "all the rage" from the late nineteenth century onward. In 1892 Professor Thaddeus S. C. Lowe, a Civil War balloonist, conceived a recreational coup which gave city residents a place to spend their idle hours. This was a gravity railroad up a sixty-two percent grade above Pasadena. On top of the mountain, Echo Peak, its passengers transferred to a more level electric line which circled several canyons to arrive at another crest appropriately named after Lowe. A tavern at the end of the line provided a favorite tourist attraction until fire destroyed it in 1936.

Less ambitious was the inclined railroad which Colonel J. W. Eddy built in 1901. This funicular line, called "Angel's Flight," ran up Bunker Hill from Third and Hill streets for one block. The ride up the hill cost only one cent. The line was dismantled in 1969 to make room for urban renewal, and the little orange cars were placed in storage, with the promise that one day "the world's shortest railway" would be rebuilt. As of 1981 this pledge had not yet been kept.

High-flown descriptions of the city's suburbs were also designed to lure readers throughout America to a land of blue skies and orange groves. Partly as a result of this massive advertising, the suburbs of Los Angeles experienced a "health rush" that resembled the gold rush of an earlier day. Mineral springs, spas, and health resorts advertised their "fresh air" atmosphere, inviting tuberculars and other invalids to Tujunga, Sierra Madre, Altadena, and Monrovia. These surrounding towns became the sanitariums of the Pacific Coast.[3] The Mediterranean climate, extolled in railroad brochures and chamber of commerce blurbs, was advertised throughout the world. Since the 1890s snowbound easterners, who heard about a Rose Parade in Pasadena each January, have been lured by the thousands to this golden land of the orange and of spring eternal. Nearby Long Beach became in these years a kind of Iowa on the Pacific. But the center of this pot of gold at the end of the rainbow was Los Angeles. Through its portals the railroads deposited their human cargo. The rainbow's rays ended in the rail yards of downtown "L.A."

In 1898 J. M. Guinn, one of the city's first historians, wrote: "Time, flood, and the hated gringos have long since obliterated all ancient landmarks and boundary lines of the old pueblo." His generation, however, did not yet know the term megalopolis. By the turn of the century southern California's hordes of new residents had wiped out forever its frontier characteristics. In 1900, Karl Baedeker's well-known tourist guidebook, *The United States, with an Excursion into Mexico,* noted that Los Angeles had a population of 102,489. Its adobe houses had "given place almost entirely to stone and brick business blocks and tasteful wooden residences." In this gleaming new city of the West, a strong agricultural economy and increasingly urban society had entered a period of fuller development.

CHAPTER SIX

Agriculture, Oil, Harbors, and Water

THE CITY'S first commerce had been agricultural. Following the gold rush of 1848–1849, the growth of population furnished an urgent market for cattle, grain, and other foodstuffs. Prior to 1860, fully sixty percent of California's population was engaged in mining, but the southern counties, of which Los Angeles was the center, became the agricultural suppliers of this moneyed population. Cattle had sold for as high as $500 per head in 1850, and the great ranchos of the south flourished. Los Angeles reigned as "Queen of the Cow Counties" until drought conditions and falling prices in the 1860s damaged the sheep and cattle industries.

Grain, wheat, fruit, and grape production also made Los Angeles important agriculturally. As early as the 1830s the town had about 100 acres of vineyards, including the vines of Luis (or Louis) Vignes, a Frenchman after whom a downtown street has been named. Unfortunately, the "mission variety" of grape did not help Vignes to produce wine of high quality. From the mid-1840s onward, within Los Angeles itself, William Wolfskill joined Vignes in experimenting with the growing of grapes and oranges. The Camulos Rancho, on the route to Ventura, was also renowned for its vines and fruit trees long before the gold rush occurred.

Another important part of the local economy was built upon cultivation of the orange. The Franciscans had realized that both climate and soil were favorable for citrus when they introduced trees into their gardens. In 1804, they planted one of the earliest groves at San Gabriel Mission, but their trees were scrawny by today's standards. Vignes successfully transplanted some thirty-five of the mission orange trees as well as some English walnuts. During the 1870s a much better Washington Navel variety was introduced from Brazil. This seedless fruit attracted immediate attention because of its juicy flavor. Production spread so widely that by 1872 there were 35,000 orange trees in Los Angeles County. Five years later, soon after railroad service became available, Wolfskill's family sent the first trainload of oranges eastward to St. Louis. The fruit arrived in good condition and found a favorable market. Soon other Los Angeles growers were sending carloads eastward and exploring the possibilities of advertising.

One of the orange industry's primary concerns was the quest for larger markets. In 1893, growers founded the Southern California Fruit Growers Exchange. Later they expanded and encouraged that cooperative's marketing throughout the state. Its trade name, "Sunkist," became nationally known. In attempting to change the American breakfast diet, growers sent specially decorated trains eastward to distribute free oranges at whistle stops. They also experimented with new methods of production and packaging. In time millions of boxes of oranges were shipped annually to the East. Increased production of lemons further rounded out citriculture.

Along with citrus growers and real-estate developers, "L.A." attracted retired businessmen, often from the Midwest, who built hotels, formed travel firms, and organized service companies. Invalids, too, found a restorative life in the sunshine; many of them brought both capital and business experience into the city and its hinterland.

The new industry added immeasurably to the commercial stability of Los Angeles. With the development of large-scale wine production at nearby Cucamonga, egg production in the San Fernando Valley, and a big dairy industry at Norwalk, Los

Harvesting grain in the San Fernando Valley about 1900. (*C.C. Pierce Collection; by courtesy of the Huntington Library, San Marino, California.*)

Angeles achieved agricultural maturity well before the twentieth century. The city became a leading marketing center for a wide diversity of crops, including, besides oranges and lemons, apricots, peaches, almonds, walnuts, truck vegetables, figs, avocados, poultry, grain, alfalfa, livestock, and dairying. The outstanding success of the orange growers in cooperative farm marketing encouraged others. The California Walnut Growers' Association, as well as avocado and lemon farmers, established headquarters for their associations (called exchanges) in or near Los Angeles.[1]

However, agriculture steadily yielded large areas of fertile land formerly devoted to crops and livestock to real-estate subdivisions and commercial establishments. Los Angeles County's status as a leading center of agricultural production slipped eventually. Indeed, in time the orange orchards and vineyards became fixtures of the past.

Early manufacturing was chiefly for local needs and included soap, confectioneries (utilizing locally grown sugar beets), and

L. Lichtenberger's carriage factory, 147–149 Main Street, Los Angeles, 1883. (*C. C. Pierce Collection; by courtesy of the Huntington Library, San Marino, California.*)

brewing, as well as household goods. The growth of Los Angeles as a manufacturing city involved the shifting of leadership from San Francisco. In 1900 San Francisco ranked first among California's manufacturing cities but by 1910 had shown little increase in output. Los Angeles had advanced about a hundred percent in the same decade.

Yet another new source of income, stemming from the discovery of oil and tar, created a contrasting skyline of rickety derricks set amid waving palm trees. As we have seen from the descriptions of James Ohio Pattie, asphalt, or *brea,* from the tar pits west of Los Angeles was used for roofing from at least the 1820s onward. But the sustained success of the Los Angeles oil industry dates from the 1890s. Its first acknowledged leader, Edward L. Doheny, came to Los Angeles in 1892. Near Westlake Park he leased a lot out of which oozed a sticky oil seepage. At the 600-foot level one of Doheny's several wells began to produce forty-five barrels per day. This started an oil boom that

led to the digging of 2300 wells in Los Angeles within the next
five years. Ugly black derricks were even erected in back yards.

Still another rich field within the city was found in today's
Hancock Park, astride La Brea Pits. During the digging, the
bones of prehistoric animals were exhumed. Rancho La Brea's
fossil deposits are located on Wilshire Boulevard between
Ogden and Curson streets; the park was named for the Hancock family, who gave the land to the city as a scientific monument. The park has been landscaped with plants to augment the
prehistoric scene, with life-size facsimile skeletons on the site.

All of this frenzied exploration created a surplus of unsalable
oil. The product was used to keep pipes from rusting as well as
to dampen down dusty roads. Only when railroad locomotives
were converted to oil did a sizable new market for the excess
fuel emerge. By 1901 both the Southern Pacific and Santa Fe
railroads had changed from coal to fuel oil. The end of the
bicycle and horse-drawn age accompanied development of the
internal combustion engine for automobiles, which led to a demand for even larger quantities of gasoline and other petroleum
products.

In the 1920s great new oil discoveries in the Los Angeles
basin took place. One of the largest finds was in 1920 at Huntington Beach, and in 1921 other fields were developed at Santa
Fe Springs and Signal Hill. The well-known oil companies of
today soon began to emerge. From 1900 to 1930 the oil industry, despite uncertain origins and national management scandals,
took a long step toward maturity. It was spurred by the further
discovery of new pools, by improvements in refining techniques, and by growing demands for fuel.

On the sea as well as on land, transportation was at the heart
of Los Angeles's success. Out of the old and deficient port of
San Pedro there slowly emerged an enlarged Los Angeles Harbor. From 1851 to 1858 Phineas Banning had operated a wharf
and warehouse there, on an inlet sheltered by a rock jetty
between Terminal and Dead Man's islands. By 1890, when Los
Angeles was on its way toward becoming the largest city in
California, only one deficiency threatened to halt this expansion—the lack of a suitable harbor. Ships still docked at the
windy and badly exposed roadstead of San Pedro–Wilmington,
which was surrounded by mudflats, sand hills, and dank sloughs.

"Spudding-in" ceremony at Ramsey and Bemus Oil Well, Compton, 1926. (*Courtesy Security Pacific National Bank.*)

It was clear that local funds alone could not build the expensive docks, seawalls, slips, and passages necessary for a modern harbor. Some maintained that private interests should manage

actual construction of a deep harbor. Since two sites, San Pedro–
Wilmington and Santa Monica, were available, a bitter fight
developed over the future location of an expanded harbor. The
Huntington interests favored construction of a deep harbor at
Santa Monica, principally because the Southern Pacific con-
trolled all the railroad approaches to that location. They lobbied
for a $4 million facility. Angelenos, however, knew that if
Congress should select Santa Monica, their future harbor would,
in effect, be a port constructed for the benefit of Collis P.
Huntington and his company.

Determined to forestall the awarding of federal funds to Santa
Monica, an aroused Los Angeles citizenry organized a Free
Harbor League whose object was to secure the appropriation
for San Pedro. The term "free harbor" sprang from the feeling
that the new port should not be dominated by the railroad. The
Terminal Railroad, a minor competitor of the powerful Southern Pacific, had access to San Pedro. This gave Los Angeles at
least some assurance that access to its future harbor would not
be the exclusive province of the Huntington monopoly. Critics
of the Southern Pacific felt that if Huntington got his way, the
SP would set whatever freight rates it wanted, and thus govern
the loading and unloading of harbor cargo. Senator Stephen W.
White allied himself with the Free Harbor Leaguers, as did the
Los Angeles Times and the city's chamber of commerce, under its
energetic secretary, Charles Dwight Willard. Senator White, a
vigorous and persuasive orator, battled from 1893 to 1896 to
prevent Huntington from achieving his goal of having the federal funds allocated to Santa Monica. The "free-harbor" fight
ended with San Pedro being designated as the site of Los
Angeles's port, again epitomizing the distrust of the Southern
Pacific that had been built up in the public mind.

In 1896 Congress appropriated $2.9 million for major harbor
construction, and in 1899 the city celebrated a "Free Harbor
Jubilee." Some twenty thousand persons gathered at San Pedro
to watch the dumping of the first bargeload of stone for a breakwater.[2] This harbor project was one of the most significant
engineering achievements of Pacific Coast history. United States
War Department engineers constructed a protective breakwater
which, by 1912, jutted out into the ocean 11,152 feet. Eventually this rock-filled seawall was to extend for more than eight

miles; its outer harbor enclosed 6,000 acres of channels and anchorages. The opening of the Panama Canal in 1914 increased the amount of shipping and placed Los Angeles among the major seaports of the world. Within the next decade the city eclipsed San Francisco in total annual port tonnage. It easily became the leading port on the West Coast of both North and South America.

As Los Angeles grew, its city fathers realized that new water resources would be necessary if the city was to continue expanding. A kind of mythology has been built up about the scarcity of water. Los Angeles never actually had to seek out water to meet current needs. Instead, it was ceaselessly concerned about planning for population expansion. To satisfy its vision of the future, the city locked up vast underground rights to water which it has never used. Even today Los Angeles has not exercised its full rights to Colorado River water, relying upon the Owens River basin and other sources.

In the early 1900s civil engineers convinced local leaders that they should tap the waters of the Owens River in the southern Sierra. In actuality, the city went after these resources partly because of its anticipated need for hydroelectric power. Because of this intrusion some seventy-five years ago, a struggle began between residents of the Owens Valley and water agents who started to buy up land parcels with valuable subsoil water rights attached. With the support of President Theodore Roosevelt and Gifford Pinchot, head of the U.S. Forest Service, Los Angeles received a right-of-way across federal land. It also annexed major unincorporated areas to insure its future water needs. After Angelenos voted a $23 million bond issue in 1907, construction of one of the most controversial projects in the history of the state began with considerable efficiency. The project was an amazing system of canals, tunnels, and pipelines to carry the water. This 233-mile "water highway" included a pipeline across the Mojave Desert to transport the melted snow of the Sierra, and it was completed in only five years. Fred Eaton, an influential former mayor and city engineer, had joined forces with William Mulholland, superintendent of the city's water department. Mulholland, remarkably talented, has since come to be called "water bearer to the Angels." In his time there was profound admiration for a man so taciturn that when the

aqueduct gates were opened in 1913 to release Owens Valley
water, he uttered the terse statement: "There it is. Take it." This
was reminiscent of Brigham Young's "This is the place"—his
designation of Utah's Salt Lake Basin as the new Mormon
home. Although the aqueduct still did not reach all the way to
Los Angeles, the city held a two-day celebration that year at the
system's San Fernando spillway. The faraway *New York Times*
reported that the event drew fifteen thousand automobiles and
forty thousand spectators.

Two years later, Los Angeles annexed 168 square miles of the
San Fernando Valley. Critics alleged that this move was to aid a
syndicate headed by Harry Chandler of the *Los Angeles Times,*
General Otis's son-in-law. This group had reputedly acquired
almost fifty thousand acres of land in the valley with a view to
siphoning off cheap surplus water. Whether this allegation was
true or not, the *Times* did feature in its columns the water
shortages which the city allegedly faced. In 1904, upon learning
of the Los Angeles Water Board's plans to tap the waters of the
Owens Valley, the paper actually predicted a water famine, an
apparent attempt to quell criticism of the controversial project.
Critics maintained that the *Times* group of investors reaped
$120 million from an outlay of only $2.5 million and that this
was the foundation of the Chandler fortune. Later Harry
Chandler was called the biggest landowner in southern California.[3]

The new Owens Valley conduits provided Los Angeles with
four times as much water as the city then needed. This only
encouraged the howls of angry ranchers and farmers further
north. Those forced to evacuate their homes in the area south of
Bishop and Inyokern remained permanently angry, contribut-
ing to the reputation of Los Angeles as a looter of water—this,
despite the reimbursements of money which the city made to
those whose properties had been usurped.[4]

While developing its water resources, Los Angeles also pioneered in building long-distance transmission lines. Because
coal was not readily available, electric power generated in surrounding mountain areas added invaluable energy to the city's
industrial growth.

The city of Los Angeles eventually came to own a quarter
million acres of land in the Owens basin. Critics averred that its

water diversion operations would not only deplete the area's native vegetation but that local farms would virtually cease to exist. Even while the Owens Valley controversy raged, Los Angeles and nearby communities again complained about inadequate supplies of both water and hydroelectric power.

By 1928 Congress passed a law to permit construction of a dam in Boulder Canyon (eventually built in Black Canyon) on the Colorado River several hundred miles east of Los Angeles. This project, undertaken jointly by the federal government with other southwestern states and local municipalities, was designed to protect the Imperial Valley against flooding, provide a multistate water reserve, and generate still more hydroelectric energy for the entire Southwest. Los Angeles became the keystone metropolis of this important effort. Hoover Dam, completed in 1936, dwarfed the Owens River Aqueduct. The dam provided a lifeline of water without which southern California could not have expanded as it did. Fortunately, the Boulder Canyon Project had been completed before World War II broke out.

By the 1950s the city and nearby communities were once more talking about the need to develop new sources of water. California's water problems had become ensnarled in a north-south sectional controversy over retention of water rights by northern "counties of origin." These were reluctant to release further water resources to an insatiable Los Angeles. Construction of the controversial and vital Feather River Project finally commenced in 1960. In the next decade Los Angeles received a new infusion of water.

CHAPTER SEVEN

A New Political and Economic Base

FOLLOWING A SERIES of San Francisco municipal scandals in 1906, Los Angeles alerted itself to the need for political housecleaning. The city participated in a national "Progressive revolt" that occurred when President Theodore Roosevelt and other critics spoke out vigorously for reform. In Los Angeles a group of young local reformers won a key municipal election in 1906 and then a year later helped launch the Lincoln-Roosevelt League. They worked through it to drive corruption and graft out of government. Indeed, Los Angeles, via the influence of a public-spirited physician, John R. Haynes, became one of the first cities in the nation to adopt the initiative, referendum, and recall.[1] Its electorate soon recalled Mayor Arthur C. Harper, who had received the support of the Southern Pacific railroad's political machine while running for office. Harper, exposed as involved in a sugar stock speculation, had the dubious honor of being the first public official in the United States ever to be recalled. This exposé came at a time when a still obscure San Francisco prosecutor, Hiram Johnson, was planning the political derailment of the Southern Pacific's supposedly invincible political machine. Johnson, because of his successes, went on to win the governorship in 1910.

Because the reform-minded citizens of Los Angeles were once so eager to decentralize political power, the city in our day has come to be governed by an archaic charter that dates from its progressive reform era. It provides for severe limitations upon the powers of elected officials. The mayor became responsible for law enforcement, the appointment of city officers, supervision of departments, and preparation of the budget. But his control over other city officials remained purposely weak. The municipal policy-making body, then and today, is the city council. It is responsible for the budget, taxes, assessments, public improvements, and civil service employees. The charter was drafted according to the doctrine that the weaker any unit of government, the less harm it can do.

Some city departments remain virtually autonomous, still authorized by the charter to obtain revenues separately from the rest of the city's government. Such departments have jurisdiction over recreation and parks, water and power, the harbor, and airports. Many other functions and offices fall under budgetary control of the mayor and city council. As to the county, it is, in the number of officials it employs, the largest county government in the nation. This colossus, furthermore, straddles 4,060 square miles of jurisdiction. A tangled mass of government agencies divides the metropolitan area, saps its strength, and threatens the mobility upon which its eighty-one satellite communities depend. This contrived looseness of government— with its strange alliance of disparate centers—has become symbolic of Los Angeles itself.

As to reform, the Progressives established a pattern that still exists. Ambivalence is at its core. The city fell into the Progressives' habit of opting for change while seeking to conserve such old-fashioned values as private enterprise, regional patriotism, and isolationism. The result was pseudo-reform. City-owned utilities were combined with a conservative resistance to making deeper governmental changes. Makeshift improvisations hardly created an ideal urban laboratory for city government. A frontier mentality long dominated realistic adaptation to future growth. The demand for low taxes impeded progress toward creation of a beautiful modern city with adequate parklands and intelligent planning.

The small-mindedness of both voters and leaders seemed endemic. In a generation whose center seemed rooted in materialism and private gain, Colonel Griffith J. Griffith provided a surprising exception. In 1896 he donated to the city over three thousand acres of hilly and wooded acreage for a park. Sixteen years later he gave $100,000 for the building of an observatory. By then Los Angeles had incorporated Griffith Park within its boundaries and had added a thousand acres to create one of the nation's largest city parks.

In providing the social setting within which this particular city grew, the *Los Angeles Times* has had an especially important role. The *Times,* successor of the *Star,* was acquired in 1881 by an easterner, General Harrison Gray Otis, whose rank came from national guard service during the Spanish-American War. His daughter married Harry Chandler, an energetic young newspaperman. Ownership of the *Times* eventually passed into the hands of the Chandlers, their children and grandchildren. The Otis-Chandler family combine saw its role as that of southern California's voice—as promoters of business and as advocates of regional expansion and population growth. Via real-estate promotion, power brokerage (with a conduit into city hall), irrigation and water schemes, and antilabor as well as antireform advocacy, the *Times* became the single most important private and public influence within Los Angeles except for government itself. [2]

The paper became embroiled in a number of significant civic issues—among them the already-mentioned Free Harbor struggle, the Owens River water controversy, and violent union difficulties. On October 1, 1910, extremist elements in the labor movement bombed the *Times;* the explosion was so powerful that it was heard more than ten miles away. Twenty persons were killed and many more injured; out of the rubble of this disaster arose the even more adamant conservative editorial philosophy of the *Times.* Abrasive tension between the paper and labor organizers had been of long duration. After the bombing, mutual suspicion increased even more. General Otis blamed irresponsible members of the International Association of

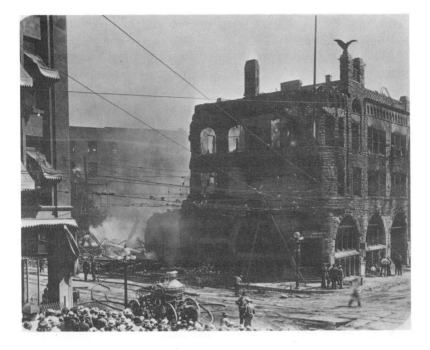

Destruction by fire of Los Angeles Times Building, 1910. Firemen can be seen trying to save the structure. (*Photo is by C. C. Tarter in the C. C. Pierce Collection; by courtesy of the Huntington Library, San Marino, California.*)

Bridge and Structural Iron Workers for the tragedy. Conversely, labor denied that a bomb had caused the blast and accused the *Times* of criminal negligence in operating a plant which union spokesmen called a gas-leaking firetrap. Only after a lengthy trial was the incident established as an act of union violence.

In 1911 three agitators were brought to trial and accused of organizing the bombing. Labor leaders retained the renowned attorney Clarence Darrow to defend them. Testimony against the defenders was, however, too incriminating for Darrow to win their acquittal. The good offices of the crusading journalist Lincoln Steffens were used to arrange a mysterious compromise by which the defendants changed their pleas to guilty, apparently in exchange for the prosecution dropping pursuit of other suspects. Although the offenders were imprisoned, public opinion denounced unions as did, of course, the *Times*. The bombing temporarily quelled the militancy of the labor movement in Los

Angeles. The city became an open-shop town, but the unrest of workers continued to fester.

Meanwhile, the *Times* and its merchant constituency flourished during World War I when labor was prevented from striking for higher wages and shorter working hours. Then came a vast immigration into the city during the 1920s which accompanied the advent of the automobile. This was yet another boom period—resembling the 1849 gold rush and the real-estate craze of the mid-1880s. Real-estate promoters once again sold lots that became new suburbs virtually overnight. The renewal of massive promotional campaigns attracted thousands upon thousands of people into the municipalities surrounding Los Angeles. With water assured, the city inexorably fanned out into its hinterland. By the 1930s a vast accumulation of people was changing Los Angeles from a farm and ranch community into the largest urban center on the West Coast. Sheep, goats, and chicken coops were giving way to back-yard barbecues and swimming pools.

With the automobile as its main linkage, the city fragmented and decentralized itself while it grew. As if to forecast what the future American city would be like, Los Angeles established an amorphous, Balkanized pattern of growth. The aspirations and fears of other metropolises were first actualized here, particularly as to transportation. Fortunately, during the interwar years Los Angeles was connected by the Pacific Electric Railroad system's "Big Red Cars," which no longer exist.

The clang of bells from the "P.E.'s" cars could be heard at every major intersection. Its network covered eleven thousand miles, the cars sometimes traveling at speeds close to fifty miles per hour, mostly on private right-of-ways. A commuter could ride from Pasadena to Los Angeles over the "short line" within half an hour. One could go from the center of Los Angeles to Redondo Beach in forty-five minutes and from Santa Monica to Los Angeles in as little as twenty minutes, with no traffic signals and only a few station stops enroute. New towns sprang up alongside the sprawling networks of tracks and telephone poles that carried the electric power for the "Big Red Cars." Between 1920 and 1925 lots at the Carthay Center sold on the strength that they were located "fourteen minutes by red car from Per-

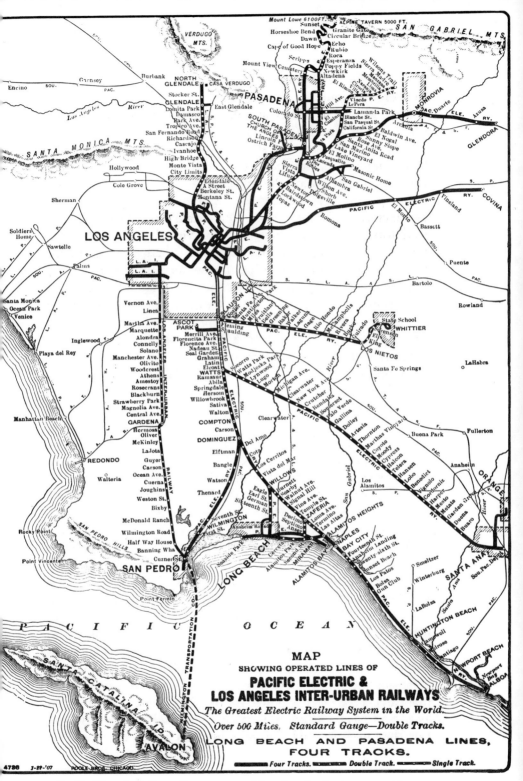

Pacific Electric Railway System map of Los Angeles basin, 1907. (*Courtesy Security Pacific National Bank.*)

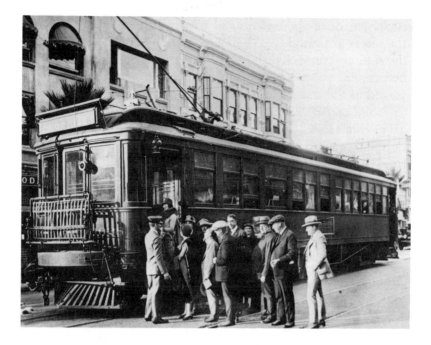

One of the "Big Red Cars" of the Pacific Electric Railway system, shown in the 1920s. (*Courtesy Security Pacific National Bank.*)

shing Square." In those years a hundred thousand people a year were arriving in Los Angeles. The bean fields of Beverly Hills and Brentwood were filling in with tract houses.

Freight, too, moved rapidly to and from the center of the city via the Pacific Electric Connection with the Wilmington and San Pedro port area. In 1906 the problem of "L.A.'s" access to the sea had been solved by the city's annexation of a strip of land about twenty miles long and a quarter mile wide. Known as the "shoestring corridor," this passageway still connects the central city with San Pedro and Wilmington, part of the greater harbor. Both communities were consolidated with Los Angeles. So the inland city of Los Angeles acquired a port of its own. Since World War II Long Beach has become a daring rival of San Pedro by using its substantial oil revenues to contruct modern port facilities. Together these ports handle more commerce than any other harbor on the West Coast.

Just as Los Angeles had provided for an expanded water

supply, it developed additional transportation facilities during the interwar period. By 1940 a new freeway (among the first in the nation) connected the civic center with Pasadena. The year before, an expanded rail terminal, Union Station, opened; it served as the transport center of the city before World War II. Combining Moorish and Spanish architecture, this terminal gave visitors their first sight of Los Angeles. The palace-like building was crowded and noisy, but gradually aviation and truck traffic were to sidetrack the many trains that originated or completed their journeys there.

Preoccupation with the automobile was central to Los Angeles's growth. Form did, indeed, follow function as Los Angeles sprawled. The year 1934 saw the first drive-in movie theater. This was followed by drive-in milk stores, banks, and restaurants, and the installation of parking meters (as late as 1949 one could park for an hour for five cents). Stores which fronted the "Miracle Mile" on Wilshire Boulevard between La Brea and Fairfax now provided parking lots adjacent to their locations.

As for air activity, in 1910 an international air show was held on the former Dominguez Ranch's flatlands. Except for the Wright brothers, it attracted the leading aeronautic pioneers in the emerging field of human flight. The event included stunt flying, hedge hopping, and even dirigible races. The barley field on which these events were staged later bore the name of Mines Field. Today the Los Angeles International Airport (LAX) sprawls out over a huge area that also encompasses the site where the Aero-Club of Southern California once held its derring-do meets. As late as December 15, 1925, the *Los Angeles Illustrated Daily News* advertised a twenty-mile flight over Los Angeles from Rogers Airport (at Western Avenue and 125th Street) for only $2.50. There were other small airfields spread throughout the city that have since disappeared.

A struggling infant aircraft industry was soon to be hit by the ten-year national economic depression that began in 1929. This brought thousands of unemployed to Los Angeles. Displaced from America's "dust bowl" areas, some of them eventually found work in aircraft construction. The outbreak of World War II provided the city with a new industrial stimulus. Because of its ideal flying weather, numerous aviation manufacturers had already located their plants in the vicinity. The Douglas and

Mines Field airport in 1933 (later part of Los Angeles International Airport [LAX]). (*Courtesy Security Pacific National Bank.*)

Lockheed plants became cornerstones of American air power. At the height of the war Lockheed employed a work force of ninety thousand persons. Consolidated Vultee, North American, Northrop, and Hughes aircraft companies also expanded during the 1940s.

Southern California became a vast staging area for the war effort in the Pacific, ideal for testing both airplanes and troop readiness. The shipyards at Wilmington and San Pedro expanded, as did air bases at March Field, El Toro, and China Lake. The Kaiser Steel Mill at Fontana was another result of World War II, however impractical its location today in a smog-filled basin.

In 1940 the federal government had spent only $728 million (mostly for the relief of Great Depression indigents) in California. Toward the end of the war, in 1945, $35 billion in federal funds had flooded into the state, much of this money for military contracts. A by-product of these expenditures was the development of high technology hardware, which increased even more dramatically when victory over Japan was achieved.[3] Indeed, the Los Angeles basin was to become one of the nation's foremost space-age laboratories as the former airframe industry diversified into radar, missiles, and jet equipment production. New terms came into use to help explain the technocratic society about to emerge; among these were the words "aerospace electronics" and "R & D." The universities were enlisted in this research and, after hostilities came to an end, new institutions emerged that combined the efforts of industry and academia. An example was the Jet Propulsion Laboratory, funded by the federal government for the California Institute of Technology in nearby Pasadena. In Santa Monica the Rand Corporation carried out research programs for various branches of the government.

The term "Federal City" came to be applied to Los Angeles as an ever closer relationship developed between its economy and the national capital. Critics averred that local industrialists and municipal leaders were more responsive to Washington contracts than to business with Sacramento. As a center of science and technology, the L.A. region was becoming the largest complex of military production in the nation. It grew to be as well known for its missiles as for its movie premières or endless real-estate speculations.

Los Angeles increasingly possessed what amounted to a "nongovernmental civil service." Aircraft, missile component, and instrument workers relied more and more upon government contracts for jobs. This made for employment vulnerability whenever "defense" expenditures were cut. The "cold war" with the Soviet Union, nevertheless, provided a steady need for military production.

Increasingly technological, Los Angeles has never been a city in decline. Nor has it reflected or mimicked traditional European (or Asian) values—as did New York and San Francisco. For mile after mile the postwar city went on replicating itself. The suburb of Lakewood exemplified this trend. In 1946, on one day alone, real-estate salesmen sold 107 homes during one hour. Every fifteen minutes building crews dug new foundation trenches. This particular development involved 3,300 acres of land and the installation of 133 miles of streets.

Arroyo Seco (Pasadena) Freeway, ca. 1948. (*Courtesy Security Pacific National Bank.*)

Despite explosive growth, the guidebooks of only forty years ago still described the nearby San Gabriel Valley as "a region of extensive citrus groves, vineyards, and truck farms." As late as 1940 Tarzana in the San Fernando Valley was "surrounded by small farms used for alfalfa growing, truck gardening, and horticulture." The word "freeway" had not yet appeared. The Arroyo Seco and later freeways were called "super modern parkways."[4] Motorized physical growth was everywhere to be seen.

A near-perfect climate before the days of smog brought corporations as well as people west. These were the years before man-made disasters. Developers did not realize they were building the slums of the future. Little did anyone in the interwar period imagine that an unfocused sprawl would insidiously destroy historic landmarks and despoil the Santa Monica Mountains. There was, furthermore, plenty of decent and affordable housing. Crime on the streets was then virtually unknown, and the public school system was not in a state of decay but growing.

Unlike San Francisco, the preoccupations of Los Angeles

have not been with tradition or history. The people who ran the
city between the two world wars looked, instead, at current
expansion. In general, civic leaders did not, however, plan especially well for an aesthetic future. Theirs was a concern with
adjustment to technology. One can see the shift toward "effi-
ciency" reflected in the city's downtown architecture. The sky-
scrapers being built in the 1980s stand in contrast to the beaux-
arts Renaissance style of the Biltmore Hotel, erected in 1923 on
Pershing Square. Flower and Figueroa streets have recently
been transformed by towering new buildings that eclipse even
the highrise structures of the 1960s. Multistoried architecture
has moved back toward the center-city, just as it had once
spread westward along the Wilshire corridor. At the opposite
end of that corridor, closer to the ocean, rises Century City, a
concentration of buildings true only to itself. Economic power
has eclipsed the traditions of the past in this city of the twentieth
century.

Between the two world wars the Mexican American heritage
(and population as well) were reduced to a marginal ethnic
enclave, subjugated to the dominant Anglo community. "La
Reina" of the past had moved beyond the local epithet "Queen
of the Cow Counties" toward congestion that was reflective of
broader national trends. The growth of Los Angeles did not
occur in a regional vacuum. One description in those years was
of a city composed of one hundred midwestern towns that each
numbered a population of ten thousand persons.

Politics, as with any other city, has been entwined with the
economic and social problems of Los Angeles—as has the role
of its mayors. We cannot review the record of every such chief
executive. One of these, however, became enmeshed in a scandal of major proportions. This was Frank L. Shaw, a former
wholesale grocery salesman and "New Dealer" who had achieved
the city's highest post. In 1938 his brother was accused of
having accepted a $15,000 bribe from underworld figures. The
city tried and convicted Joseph Shaw of civil-service fraud.
Labor violence, strikes, and additional allegations that linked
the Shaw administration with racketeers led to the mayor's
recall. Only in 1941 did the state supreme court overturn the
conviction of his brother. Meanwhile, a spirited group of reformers, led by a new mayor, Fletcher Bowron, was swept into

office. A historian has recently suggested that these reformers themselves should bear some of the blame for the scandals that occurred in Los Angeles during those years.[5]

Looking back upon the city of the interwar period, we can now see trends that were not then discernible. Los Angeles remained conservative in political and social outlook, mostly Protestant in religion, boosterish as to its future, materialist, and more than faintly racist in celebrating its Anglo values. These were the clichés uttered *sotto voce* about "L.A.," as it increasingly came to be called. We can now turn toward a consideration of how these rubrics were reflected in the general culture.

CHAPTER EIGHT

Culture
and Society

SINCE THE 1880S Los Angeles has been struggling to find
a sense of cultural unity. As it grew, perhaps its major
enticement has been climate. Attractive also was its free style of
life, exotic agriculture, easy wealth, new industry, and a hundred
ways of making a living. Herein lies one of its greatest problems—the search for a social center. The Los Angeles basin has
been filled and refilled with rootless strangers who had little in
common.

One of the first attempts to digest the Hispanic past within an
emerging Anglo pattern was the establishment in 1883 of the
Historical Society of Southern California. Its quarterly is now
the oldest in the Far West. The society has had limited support.

A strong exponent of the Indian-Spanish-Mexican heritage
was Charles Fletcher Lummis. This eccentric but brilliant Harvard classmate of Theodore Roosevelt came to Los Angeles
before the turn of the century to help advertise its characteristics. Lummis wrote and lived out a Bohemian interpretation of
Spanish colonial life at El Alisal, a residence that he constructed
with his own hands from boulders on the edge of the Arroyo
Seco. From 1895 to 1902, infatuated with the culture of Spain,
he edited *Land of Sunshine* (later *Out West*), a magazine which
extolled the Hispanic and Indian past. The colorful Lummis,
often wearing a corduroy suit, a red sash around his middle, and

a sombrero, championed the plight of the Indian, fought to save the crumbling Spanish missions, and in 1903 founded today's Southwest Museum.[1] The writings of George Wharton James and Helen Hunt Jackson also dwelt on many of the same themes.

During the generation of materialism the mission revival style of architecture reflected the change and turbulence of Los Angeles. So did the "California bungalows" built by Charles and Henry Greene, designed to adapt regional characteristics to the use of natural building materials. Their new dwellings supplanted a variety of earlier architectural styles, among them the wooden ranch houses of the late nineteenth century as well as Victorian Gothic, Queen Anne structures, and facsimile chalets.

Architectural experimentation also affected educational institutions. The first buildings of the California Institute of Technology, which began in the 1890s as the Throop Institute, were in the mission revival style. Today known popularly as Caltech, that institution grew into a center of scientific teaching and research. Associated with it is Mount Wilson Observatory, which holds a foremost place in the astronomical field. The Henry E. Huntington Library and Art Gallery, established in 1923 as a public trust, not only has drawn American and foreign scholars because of its facilities for Anglo-American literary and historical research, but also attracts thousands of visitors to its galleries and botanical gardens.

In the path of the city's westward march to the sea, the University of California at Los Angeles, especially after it occupied its Westwood campus in 1929, grew in size and importance similar to the parent campus at Berkeley. A second, but private, institution is the University of Southern California, founded in 1880, which has chosen to remain in the downtown area. Even earlier, in 1855, St. Vincent's College, today's Loyola Marymount University, was founded by the Roman Catholics. Occidental College was established in 1887. In recent years there has been a proliferation of junior colleges and state universities. Perhaps the most prominent of the former is Los Angeles City College. The California State University system has two campuses within the city limits, one in Northridge and another on the east side.

During these years Los Angeles began to pay half-hearted

attention to its historical sites. Places like La Mesa Battlefield, where the last encounter in California took place during the Mexican War, were marked with plaques. In the 1920s the city fathers refurbished the sleazy Plaza area and adjoining Olvera Street as tourist attractions. From earliest times called the "Walk of the Angels," that street is presently a brick-paved lane, usually crowded with visitors. Each Christmas the colorful ceremony of Las Posadas, telling of Mary's search for a birthplace for Jesus, is held there.

The way in which Olvera Street was rescued from grimy oblivion reminds of the role of women in promoting social and cultural growth. In 1926 Christine Sterling led a campaign to convert that decaying alleyway into what became the West's first shopping mall. It was named after Agustín Olvera, an early judge. Sterling enlisted the help of the Chamber of Commerce and the chief of police (who assigned her prison labor) in cleaning up a debris-ridden, rat-infested lane. It was dedicated as a public historical site in 1930.[2]

Caroline Severance was yet another vigorous champion of public and private causes. She arrived in Los Angeles in 1875 and helped to establish the first public library as well as a book club. Her Friday Morning Club, founded in 1891, advocated the reform of the juvenile detention system, and she led a campaign to develop a philharmonic orchestra, to save the giant sequoias, and to establish markers along what came to be known as El Camino Real, the route linking the California missions. She also established important charities and was an advocate for children and women's rights. She helped gain the vote for women, which was achieved in 1911.

Yet another woman leader was Harriet Williams Russell Strong, an agriculturist, proponent of civic causes, and water developer. In 1894 she helped to found the Ebell Club in order to enrich cultural opportunities for women. She, too, backed the cause of a municipal symphony orchestra. The guitar and fandango were bound to be replaced by other musical forms.

Often forgotten is that among the women leaders of any city, there have been minority members. An example is Biddy Mason, a former Georgia slave. She had crossed the plains in 1851 with her three daughters, driving a herd of sheep behind her master's wagon train. After achieving freedom legally, she

worked for a Los Angeles physician as midwife and nurse at
$2.50 per day. Upon his suggestion, she invested $250 in
property during the real-estate boom of 1887. She lived to see
that land soar in value to $200,000. She used her wealth for a
variety of charities, including a Negro nursery school, the pay-
ment of the expenses and taxes of her church, and aid to
indigent black families. Her home became a refuge for needy,
poor, and stranded individuals. In 1891, when she died, Biddy
Mason was one of the most affluent women in the American
West.

Slowly Los Angeles experienced the emergence of a culture
both solid and bizarre as well as impervious to criticism. In
1919, through the philanthropy of William Andrews Clark, Jr.,
the Los Angeles Philharmonic Orchestra was founded. It attracted outstanding conductors, including Otto Klemperer, Alfred Wallenstein, and Eduard van Beinum. In addition to this
orchestra, open-air concerts held at the Hollywood Bowl since
1921 have given local musicians an outlet for their talents and
encouraged nationally known artists to make Los Angeles a
permanent home.

During the first quarter of the twentieth century faddists and
cultists in profusion descended upon Los Angeles. The mild
winter climate and informal style of life encouraged gadflies
armed with ready solutions to mankind's dilemmas. While spiri-
tualism flourished, diet faddists prescribed mushroomburgers
and date milk shakes as a stimulus to virility and good health.
Religious fundamentalists also prospered in such an atmosphere.
Radio evangelism was pioneered in southern California by the
reverends Robert P. Shuler and Billy Sunday.

The most spectacular of these divines was Aimee Semple
McPherson, who operated her own radio station in order to
fight Satan. Dressed sometimes in an admiral's uniform, "Sister
Aimée," as she was called by her parishioners, used the music of
a xylophone and marimba band to arouse religious passions at
the Four Square Gospel Church. Yet she was generous beyond
belief to the downtrodden, sick, and unemployed. Sentimental
and lonely elderly persons transplanted from other parts of the
country venerated her.[3] Despite the fact that she founded over
a hundred branches of her church, visiting critics found it diffi-

cult to take seriously the Los Angeles of Sister Aimee. Only later did they discover her works of charity during the Great Depression, her devotion to the lonely and forgotten, but she remained an enigma to them.

In the years after 1930 Los Angeles began to emerge as a sports center. When the city celebrated the 150th anniversary of its founding in 1932, the occasion was marked by hosting the tenth Olympiad. The city built an impressive new coliseum in which Mildred (Babe) Zaharias, probably the greatest woman athlete in the world, performed. To bolster its self-image, the city has consistently sought out athletic talent, be it baseball teams or Olympic contests in which individuals perform. (L.A. gave a rousing welcome in 1957 to the Brooklyn Dodgers, a baseball club which it possessively renamed.)

During the interwar years construction of a series of landmarks drew attention to Los Angeles as a center of bad taste. These were hardly buildings, but originally took the form of roadside stands, made to look like what was sold within them. A doughnut shop was built into a doughnut; a hot dog stand was made to look like a hot dog, while a barbecue business assumed the shape of a pig. Some of these frivolous curiosities still exist. Among the best-known names are the Brown Derby, Tail o' the Pup, Mother Goose Pantry, the Zep diner (in the form of a Zeppelin), and Hoot Hoot I Scream, an ice-cream parlor. The Sampson Tire Company built its headquarters in the shape of an Assyrian palace. Coca-Cola constructed a bottling plant on Central Avenue that looked like an art deco ocean liner, while real-estate offices and movie houses were facsimiles of Egyptian sphinxes. If one did not view these architectural atrocities with good humor, it was possible to reach the conclusion, as did distant critics, that an age of decay had, symbolically, taken over the whole of L.A.

Fortunately the 1930s also saw more substantial material progress. In those years the first transcontinental "streamlined" passenger trains arrived and the State Building, General Hospital, and Griffith Park Observatory were built. In 1941 water from the Colorado River also reached Los Angeles.

On the eve of World War II a number of prominent foreign composers sought refuge in the area, among them Arnold Schoenberg and Igor Stravinsky. They were joined by writers as

well as by refugee artists who sought a freer environment in
which to work. They were divided into two groups—the Germans and the English. Among the former was Lion Feuchtwanger who, in 1940, escaped from a Nazi concentration camp.
He was joined by Thomas Mann, Kurt Weill, Franz Werfel, and
Bertolt Brecht. Both Schoenberg and Feuchtwanger made new
contributions in the southland and, upon their deaths, left their
libraries to local institutions. The English, who had arrived
mostly before World War II, included Christopher Isherwood,
Aldous Huxley, Evelyn Waugh, and Bertrand Russell, who for a
time taught philosophy at UCLA. Actors Ronald Colman, Charles
Laughton, and David Niven also were attracted by Hollywood.

Asked why he had settled in southern California, Huxley
once quipped: "I stopped there on my way to India, and because of inertia and apathy remained." Los Angeles nevertheless
had an influence on the way Huxley wrote. A critic of outdated
Victorian pomposities, Huxley grew cynical; yet he sought solutions that might satisfy man's animal and spiritual needs. In *After
Many a Summer Dies the Swan* (1939), Huxley mocked both
ostentation and personal hollowness. He became increasingly
impressed with eastern mystical thought and, accompanied by
Isherwood, began to attend meetings of the Vedanta cult. Both
hated the grotesquely palatial residences of the Hearsts and of
the movie magnates and lampooned advertisements for funeral
parks ("the Beverly Pantheon, a Personality Cemetery"). Huxley also experimented with mescaline, sought to improve his
visions of Buddhism, wrote about utopias, and peopled his
decreasingly popular novellas with mystics searching for God in
a semiarid paradise of orange groves and eternal sun. He stayed
on in southern California until his death in 1963. Isherwood,
too, remained behind, but Evelyn Waugh, after writing *The
Loved One* (1948), another tiresome spoof of the cemeteries,
returned to life in England, as did Russell.

These foreign satirists experienced Los Angeles as philistine,
as peculiarly hospitable to occultism, as a final frontier resting
place where odd practices and exotic practitioners were toler-
ated long after stable social patterns had become the rule elsewhere. Ideas and movements that embarrassed the rest of the
nation gave southern California a reputation for delusional behavior and an impaired sense of reality. In the individual such

conduct is associated with regression to infantile stages. In their delusions, some persons saw, heard, and even met angels as well as demons in the Los Angeles ethos. The lampooning of what looked like hallucinatory behavior became a virtual cottage industry for visiting critics. The English had begun a trend which continues.

Yogi mystics and Swami palm readers garnered such an unusual local following that they too lent themselves to ridicule. So did those fading movie queens who testified to the power of dietary cures and products, and who placed their faith in rainmakers, Hindu gurus, and occultists of all descriptions. As for the funeral parks, they remained imperishable stereotyped symbols, advertising as vales for the departed. Their stock in trade was the glossing over of the facts of death as associated with the mundane graveyard of the past. Swaddled in euphemisms, mourners are presented with a flowing vision of the hereafter as a desirable place to go, in happiness.

Meanwhile, yet another symbol of southern California had emerged which enjoyed a worldwide influence well beyond that of cemeteries and churches. Shortly after the turn of the century a chancy new form of entertainment appeared which indirectly led to the creation of an important art medium as well. This was the cinema. Almost circumstantially, Hollywood, a subdivision of Los Angeles, became the world's first film capital. The earliest filmmakers were viewed with suspicion by inhospitable local residents. They saw these newcomers as a troublesome bunch of fly-by-night entrepreneurs from the East Coast—and one step ahead of the law (specifically a New York State camera regulation). In order to avoid patent infringement litigation with Thomas Alva Edison, they had abandoned their makeshift eastern studios. In the early 1900s Angelenos scarcely imagined that these itinerants, who camped in tents while making instant pictures for nickelodeons, would become the moguls of an entire new industry. Sunshine and open space were added inducements to these innovators, who were considered undesirable in a village originally founded by Kansas prohibitionists. In a few years that rural town, which had restricted the size of sheep herds driven down Hollywood Boulevard to 2,000 head, transformed itself into a center of glitter and hype.

In 1908 Sam Selig rented a house at the corner of Olive and

Eighth streets and filmed there what has been called the first
motion picture shot in California. It was entitled *In the Sultan's
Power* and was followed by a succession of similarly vapid products. By the next year the Biograph Studios, located in a section
of the city called Edendale, had a capacity to grind out a "western" every day and a half. The Horsley brothers, called the first
Hollywood "producers," were offered five acres of land around
a barn near Hollywood and Vine streets for $4,000. They
turned down this chance to purchase what was to become prime
property because they already knew the reputation of Los Angeles realtors for inflated prices.

On the eve of World War I, Carl Laemmle, one of the pioneer
movie producers, moved his Universal Film Manufacturing
Company to North Hollywood. Films were "shot" in various
locations throughout Los Angeles. The Glassell Park district,
the Hyperion Boulevard area near Sunset, and Culver City (the
creation of Harry Culver) provided the scenery for early west-
erns or for the antics of the Keystone Kops and the Charlie
Chaplin comedies. At Pacific Palisades, near the seashore,
Thomas Ince, another producer, created Inceville, a studio
named after himself. Nearby were Venetian canals and a river
(actually La Ballona Creek). The former had been developed
south of Santa Monica as early as 1905 by Abbot Kinney who
had envisioned a Venice of America. He dredged almost twenty
miles of waterways which became extremely useful to movie
directors. Nearby, Charlie Chaplin, Mary Pickford, and Douglas
Fairbanks, among the early "stars" of the industry, eventually
formed their own company, United Artists.

In the years before World War I Los Angeles also became
the circus capital of the nation. Al G. Barnes (a Canadian whose
full name was Alpheus George Barnes Stonehouse) winter-
quartered at Palms each year. His animals were constantly used
in early motion pictures. They appeared in Metro-Goldwyn-
Mayer's logo as a lion, as camels in "desert classics," as tigers
in jungle pictures; the entire circus trains were displayed in
extravaganzas and comedies. The circus, billed as the "Largest
Wild Animal Circus in the World," was sold in the 1930s to
Ringling Brothers—Barnum and Bailey. At Barnes City (between Culver City and Venice) the first trained-seal acts were
developed. A further resource for the film industry was the

Cawston Ostrich Farms, founded in 1887 (admission twenty-five cents).[4]

The "Hollywoodizing" of Los Angeles also came to include the building of huge plaster movie theaters, among them the Million Dollar, Egyptian, Grauman's Chinese, the Wiltern, and the Carthay Circle. New fads in drinking and sexuality were set by the filmmakers. The reputation of Los Angeles as a center of sensationalism and eccentricity, as well as of scandal, dates mostly from the interwar era. As the international center for motion pictures and television, "Hollywood" has also become a synonym for tinsel glamor and hollow success.

Today, over half of the nation's motion picture and television employment is located in southern California. All major production facilities are adjacent to Los Angeles. Metro-Goldwyn-Mayer (MGM), Twentieth Century–Fox, Universal Studios (a subsidiary of MCA), Paramount, Warner Brothers, Columbia, and Walt Disney Productions, each has a production studio within thirty miles of downtown Los Angeles. Over half of the nation's allied production services are also near the studios.[5] Neverthess, today the term "Hollywood" is used to describe activities largely located outside the boundaries of that Los Angeles subdivision.

Following World War II, Los Angeles, because of its greatly increased population, needed new recreation facilities beyond those provided by the film industry. Expert opinion during the 1950s counseled that the city should increase its parks by 200 to 300 percent just to keep abreast of population growth. Having cemented over much of its potential park countryside, Los Angeles had come to rely upon synthetic rather than natural outdoor facilities. In 1957, it vigorously courted and generously provided a new home in Chavez Ravine for the Los Angeles Dodgers Baseball Club, formerly the Brooklyn Dodgers. The rationale was that this would lure more tourists to the city, and it did. More people attend Dodger games consistently than the games of any other team. Both regional universities, UCLA and USC, have joined in creating national football and baseball teams, adding to the Dodgers another dimension in sports entertainment. Disneyland, begun by Walt Disney as a children's amusement park, became the biggest tourist attraction in the West. A marine oceanarium (Marineland) at Palos Verdes on the seacoast was yet another popular tourist attraction.

A transplanted landscape has characterized the Los Angeles skyline from the year 1781 when Felipe de Neve presented the one and only plan ever to be fully implemented. Much later Frank Lloyd Wright scorned the "rag tag" architecture of the city. His designs for Hollyhock House (1917), a bold structure of Mayan inspiration, and of the Millard House (1923) in Pasadena were offered to counter a trend toward miscellaneous vulgarity. After the First World War Richard Neutra, R. M. Schindler, and Irving Gill also experimented with architectural forms then considered bold and daring. Later (1949) Wright's son, Lloyd, built the Wayfarer's Chapel at Portuguese Bend on the Palos Verdes peninsula, a glass-encased structure commissioned by the Church of New Jerusalem. The landscaped malls of today (characterized by a sameness of appearance) halfheartedly continue a type of fanciful innovation. So do alternative shopping and recreational centers, but there is a mediocre pleasantry about such modern architecture that seems to merge with the bland "international style" that, since 1945, has homogenized the world. The Los Angeles airport complex appears little different from that of Schiphol in Amsterdam. The local malls, whether in Santa Anita or Glendale (called the Galleria), resemble those in Indianapolis or Philadelphia. Their fountains, sidewalks, and trash barrels all serve the purposes of a littering consumer society. The bazaars of that "culture" are hardly beguiling monuments for the ages—whether at Los Angeles or elsewhere.

The real cultural awareness of the city gained impetus with the emergence of art museums and libraries. At Barnsdall Park (adjacent to Hollyhock House) is located a municipal art gallery, the scene also of small cultural soirées and musicales. In contrast, Westlake Park (renamed MacArthur Park in 1942) and Pershing Square have remained gathering places for oldsters and indigents who there encounter crime problems instead of rest and recreation. The Los Angeles Public Library, with many branches, houses some three million volumes. The UCLA University Research Library also supervises the William Andrews Clark, Jr., Memorial Library, a miniature Huntington Library located ten miles from the campus on Adams Boulevard. Libraries at the Los Angeles County Museum and at USC offer specialized collections on early California, the motion-picture industry, and aviation.

Growing steadily in the importance of their collections have been the Huntington Library in San Marino and the J. Paul Getty Museum at Malibu, the latter with its antiquities, including marbles, terra cottas, bronzes, and European furniture and paintings. These complement the Huntington in the field of English and American culture. In addition to a copy of the Gutenberg Bible (1455), the Huntington includes the famous "Blue Boy" painted by Thomas Gainsborough and "Pinkie" by Joshua Reynolds. The Huntington Botanical Gardens also enhance the reputation of this center for advanced literary and historical studies.

The public seems to demand more and more places to visit as an industrial society provides increased leisure time. "L.A. the tourist center" is apt to be underestimated by local residents, except when relatives come calling. Aside from Disneyland and other commercial magnets, vacationers flock toward the Griffith Park zoo, playgrounds, golf course, and observatory. Its municipal Greek Theater presents light opera and ballet. Nearby is the tiny Fern Dell Nature Museum. Not far away is the Historical Society of Southern California, located at El Alisal, formerly the home of Charles F. Lummis, writer and local eccentric.

In recent years the noncommercial radio station KPFK in Los Angeles has employed unorthodox broadcasting practices to beam cultural programs to subscription audiences. Included on their schedules are unabridged performances of plays from Aeschylus to Jean-Paul Sartre, première presentations of musical works by contemporary composers, poetry readings, and controversial discussions of present-day issues. Channel 28 (KCET), a nonprofit educational television station, performs a similar function for TV audiences.

All this activity suggests that Los Angeles has been both recipient and originator in the arts. Today's popular music and recording industry blares out its product in stadiums and clubs where, in former times, Hollywood stars were billed. Another change has been the increase in the number of performances of classical music. Local universities also draw tens of thousands of extension students to their campuses for lectures, concerts, and plays. The number of art galleries has doubled in the past ten

years, and art boosters claim there are more galleries on La
Cienega Boulevard than in all of Chicago.

The earlier farm-born conservative materialism had probably
contributed to some cultural stagnation. Later forces seemed to
change the populist shallowness of the immediate past. The first
of these was a shift in the incoming population toward more
residents with professional skills. A second factor was the growing prosperity of southern California's new industries and, third,
the emergence of a community cultural leadership with a demonstrated talent for fund-raising. Despite the influx of funds for
cultural purposes, local historical societies and theater work-
shops remained in dire financial straits.

Critics aver that a city cannot obtain a "culture" simply by
yearning for it, that Los Angeles must cling to more than un-
bridled fluidity. Direction too is necessary. It is perhaps appropriate that the Music Center is named after a member of the
Chandler family who did more to bring about its construction
than anyone else. The family's public voice, the *Los Angeles
Times,* not only had much to do with orchestrating the real-
estate booms of the 1920s and 1950s, it also immersed itself
in the neglected building of a cultural substratum. With a daily
circulation in excess of one million copies, the paper became a
coalescing factor.

One writer has suggested that sometime between the end of
World War II and the 1950s "Los Angeles acquired a sense of
identity rather than of its identities. With its highrising and
thickening center it even began to look like a city." The success
of the Music Center produced a "ripple effect" on the culture of
southern California, with artistic devotees coming from far away
to view its performances.[6] Zubin Mehta, in 1964 conductor of
the Los Angeles Philharmonic Orchestra, spoke at the dedication of the Dorothy Chandler Pavilion: "This is the most unique
city in the twentieth century. I do not think it is too late now, in
midcentury, to begin a new cultural life. This evening we are
going to usher in a new era." The pavilion was the first structure
of a cultural complex that, three years later, included the Mark
Taper Forum and Ahmanson Theater.

Visible from the downtown cloverleaf of a four-level freeway,
the buildings remind one that the central part of Los Angeles

Atlantic-Richfield Plaza, 1973. (*Courtesy Security Pacific National Bank.*)

has undergone severe redevelopment. This had included con-
struction of a convention center, a sports arena, and the new
Hotel Bonaventure, supplanting the old Biltmore on Pershing
Square as the largest in downtown Los Angeles. The three thea-
ters of the Music Center, the Atlantic-Richfield Towers, the
Security Pacific Bank complex of buildings, and the highrise

apartments on Bunker Hill seemed to further the feeling of "identity." More than thirty buildings also arose in a civic center that housed federal, state, county, and city government agencies. Resident repertory, ballet, and opera companies, as well as nineteen symphony orchestras, have also emerged. In 1965 a new Los Angeles County Art Museum was completed at Hancock Park on Wilshire Boulevard. That particular avenue has become a long corridor of glass and metal highrise buildings that mingle commercial and cultural facilities—the Park Avenue of Los Angeles.

Since the mid-1960s a measure of cultural leadership within the state has shifted from north to south. In the 1960s funds were raised for a California Institute of Arts (in essence a private university of the fine arts) and for a museum of the communications industry. Los Angeles also became the nation's second biggest national book-buying and art-collecting market. Indeed, a new generation of "business collectors," among them Norton Simon and J. Paul Getty, emerged. Like Henry E. Huntington in an earlier day, they named museums after themselves. Getty, Simon, and other serious art devotees also saw their collections as both status symbol and investment. For them what had begun as private hobby became public venture.

During 1980 a group of planners convened to consider building a new Museum of Modern Art near the Music Center on Bunker Hill. Their statement read: "We want a world-class museum . . . that will act as a focal point for a revitalized downtown area, with some of the liveliness of the Beaubourg Center in Paris." [7]

In the light of all these civic developments, it has become more difficult to charge that Los Angeles encourages privatism at the expense of community. Yet there was a time when the flight from "auto city" drove actress Mary Pickford into the hills as, in later years, it did Frank Zappa, whose electronic music for a time so stimulated the masses who lived in the flatlands below. Today their preference has shifted to "country western" performers.

Although the "culture" of Los Angeles once seemed unstructured and garish, the vitality of its artistic scene can no longer be denied. This, despite the fact that magazines, newspapers, and books continue to satirize the area as a superficial "land of pop and honey." The city that has played host to Stravinsky and Brecht today finds itself in the midst of its biggest era of cultural excitation.

This cultural growth comes at the very time when the city remains under attack, partly for shrugging off eastern chic. Neil Simon, who tried living and working in Los Angeles, could not resist calling it "Paradise with a lobotomy" in his play *California Suite* (1977). The images of kookism, kinky sexuality, and the "unusualness" of Los Angeles's fires, floods, earthquakes, and mudslides apparently will not die without a struggle. Excesses of taste and emotion are at the heart of indictments against the area. The vision of old women wearing mink, sunglasses, and slacks at poolside irks the newcomers as well as the easterners, who may view them on their TV screens.

A more realistic aspect of local "culture" was symbolized by the influx of thousands of scientists and engineers, drawn first by the aircraft industry and more recently by electronics and missiles establishments. These newcomers introduced a different intellectual orientation. The Rand (Research and Development) Corporation at Santa Monica—a semipublic, nonprofit agency that carries on long-range strategic studies by "brainstorming techniques"—brings together political scientists, physicists, and mathematicians. This amalgam is labeled a "think tank," or "R&D" intellectual "industry." Similar to the Rand Corporation but more technical in scope is the work of the Space Technology laboratories at nearby Canoga Park, the overseers of the United States Air Force's Ballistic Missile Division. Hughes Aircraft and International Telephone and Telegraph are among companies with still other specialized research facilities. The Standard Oil Company of California has established at La Habra a California Research Corporation whose exclusive activity is the pursuit of new scientific knowledge, both primary and applied.

Despite all these specialized activities and achievements, critics continue to fault the failure of Los Angeles to develop a definable urban personality. Some have spoken of an accelerated pituitary growth that makes it no more a real city than the Austro-Hungarian state was an empire. Yet both are historical realities, vast and amorphous ones. By transplanting institutions and patterns from elsewhere, citizens of the area sometimes replicated unsuccessfully what they had known before. Sometimes the resultant unlikely mixture caused the central city to lose out to its suburbs in the clash between private motives and civic betterment.

If there is anything that seems unique about Los Angeles, it is its way of life: relaxed, but energetic; open-aired, but well housed; materially advanced, yet traditional. Its people have come from everywhere, but most of them seem content to remain in the southland. Others hold tenaciously to their roots as they rejoice in the promised land.

CHAPTER NINE

Ethnic Mix

BENEATH ALL ITS frenzied growth Los Angeles encountered some trouble spots. Few communities of the late twentieth century have escaped turmoil born of social and racial tensions. World War II greatly added to the number of black residents who flocked into southern California. During the early 1960s, when the black population was growing extensively in the south-central areas of the city, its political representation remained limited. Residents of Watts or Inglewood could not then have imagined that Thomas Bradley (until 1961 a police lieutenant) would become the first black mayor of Los Angeles or that Yvonne Braithwaite Burke would become a congresswoman.

Less dispersed than any other ethnic group, young blacks who lived in the suburb of Watts had grown increasingly impatient about the discrimination and police brutality which they claimed to experience. In the heat of August 1965 a violent uprising broke out on the streets of Watts. Hundreds of disenchanted rioters, shouting anti-white epithets ("Burn Baby Burn" and "Get Whitey") looted stores, set fire to buildings, and shot at firemen and police. These enraged outbursts underscored a sense of hopelessness that grew out of economic imbalance which both the city and county later sought (rather ineffectively) to rectify.[1]

Other minorities grew to resent the social and economic inequalities to which they were subjected. Among these were the Latinos of Hispanic origin, crowded for generations into a barrio named "Sonora Town." From the 1870s onward, Mexican immigrants began to enter a society that had become Anglo in character. Despite this shift in the nature of the population, after 1916 a large number of such migrants arrived in southern California. This in-migration was a steady one throughout the 1920s. At Los Angeles the isolation of foreign-born Mexicans, residentially and socially, became apparent even within the Spanish-speaking community itself. Native-born Californios (called *pocho-cholos* by the foreign-born Mexicans) segregated themselves. Members of the older resident Hispanic population called each other *gente del país,* or people of the country, and they were seen as standoffish by the newcomers from Mexico. Those already in residence "used to treat us," one such person recalled, "as the gringos did, as dirty Mexicans." [2]

During the Second World War, labor shortages were so severe that aliens from across the border readily found jobs if not social acceptance. After the war they increasingly entered by illegal means. By the 1950s they were arriving by the tens of thousands, first as seasonal farm workers, then as permanent residents. César Chávez, who organized the earliest waves of such workers into the United Farm Workers, eventually came to see the flood of undocumented workers as a threat to his unionization struggle.

Some of these later immigrants moved toward the cities, and especially to Los Angeles, seeking jobs. In a new urban ghetto, these Latinos were employed as kitchen help or as garment workers under sweatshop conditions. Their economic status, however, was protected by federal minimum wage legislation, whether they were documented or undocumented workers. Yet many members of this cheap and willing labor pool, like those who had preceded them, felt themselves to be marginal to both the Anglo and Mexican societies. Little wonder that, politically, this minority was slow to "get its act together." Little did these people realize that the city which they founded would become one of the centers of a great ethnic struggle.

As many as a million undocumented workers have entered the United States in any given recent year. Large numbers of them have settled in the East Los Angeles area, well beyond the original enclave near the Plaza. Unfortunately, in the popular mind, they are frequently linked with criminal gang activities reported in the public press. Also, there is now yet another generational gap between the older, established Mexican Americans who arrived prior to World War II and younger Chicanos. No one deplores the acting-out of young street people more than their senior relatives, whom the young sometimes label "Tío Tacos," an epithet parallel to "Uncle Tom."

The identity problem of young Chicanos is related to their educational difficulties. The average number of school years completed by an Anglo child is 12.1 years; for a black youngster it is 9 years, but for the Mexican American only 7.1 years. Defensiveness, thus, has understandably surfaced, whether in dealing with school authorities or with the police. Young Chicanos, once labeled "Mexicans," clamor for status and a more positive visibility. Increasing numbers of them have moved toward college training and have entered the professions, including politics. Among these is Dr. Julian Nava, who became a university professor, then president of the Los Angeles school board, and later was appointed ambassador to Mexico during the administration of President Jimmy Carter.

Los Angeles is no longer a sleeping ethnic giant. Today it contains the world's largest concentration of persons of Mexican origin outside Mexico City itself. Almost four million persons of Hispanic background (including increasing numbers of Guatemalans, Cubans, and Ecuadorians) are now estimated to be in California. Perhaps a million and a half of these live within Los Angeles. There may be as many as a million and a half illegal Latino immigrants in Los Angeles County alone; city authorities believe that there are at least four hundred thousand of these undocumented aliens within the city limits. The heaviest concentrations of Mexicn Americans are in the area from the central city southeast to El Monte. East Los Angeles, Montebello, Echo Park, Lincoln Heights, Whittier, and Walnut Park also have large Latin populations. But from Santa Monica to Azusa, Latinos have also been settling in affluent and formerly "American" areas.[3]

This shift in the population pattern is especially noticeable in business areas where two languages, Spanish and English, are increasingly used for store signs, ethnic graffiti, restaurant menus, and traffic instructions. Food habits and the arts also have been affected by social change as well. *Zoot Suit,* the first Mexican-American musical play, opened at Los Angeles in 1979 and was highly successful (but closed on New York's Broadway after a disappointing one-month run, despite an expensive promotional campaign aimed at the Hispanic community). Uniquely local, the play described the notorious Sleepy Lagoon murder case and Zoot Suit Riots of June 1943 during World War II.

In that earlier period serious housing, educational, and assimilation problems surfaced. Youthful Mexican Americans demonstrated against being forced to accept inferior jobs at low wages or to remain unemployed. They clung increasingly to their language, clustered within their own clubs, and manifested separate tastes and outlooks. Called *pachucos* by their critics, they got into trouble with the police, fought on the streets of East Los Angeles, and were accused of carrying switchblade knives in trouser pockets and razor blades in their long hair. This symptomatic culture clash reminded the public that the barrios nursed deep resentments by Latinos against discrimination.[4]

As mentioned earlier, Los Angeles in the postwar period sought to attract a major baseball team to the city. The invitation to the Brooklyn Dodgers, however, required the displacement of an entire ethnic community located in Chavez Ravine. The city had itself received the land from the federal government; it was to be used "for public purposes." The Hispanics who lived on the 300 acres deeded to the Dodgers were a minor factor in the negotiations and criticisms of the project. The objections which were raised mostly concerned the expenditure of almost $5 million of public funds to improve and to grade the land as well as to build roads leading to today's Dodger Stadium. In 1957 most Angelenos considered it a significant coup to attract a National League baseball club to Los Angeles. In the litigation that ensued (the city appealed a Superior Court nullification of the contract with the Dodgers to the state supreme court), a major concern was the legality of a contract. Whatever rights the Hispanic residents of Chavez Ravine may have had were not considered.[5] Today, in an age of heightened ethnic awareness, it would be more difficult to thwart the wishes of residents who wanted to live on the land.

Only later, however, did the noncomplaining Mexican Ameri-

F
902.3
A653
1988

9.95   5/5/89

31 MAY

Chicanos. In 1970 a tragic event stirred the roots. This was the killing of Ruben Salazar, a *nes* reporter, who was accidentally shot while .tiwar rally in East Los Angeles of a group called National Moratorium. The shooting coincided with n the "Brown Berets," a militant group of young were protesting continuance of the unpopular Vietnam

1970s saw a further upsurge of community pride among anos. At Lincoln Park, a "Plaza de la Raza" commemorates presence of several million Spanish-speaking persons within s Angeles County. Currently 25 percent of all births in California involve parents of Mexican heritage. A third of all children in kindergarten schools are of such origin. Bilingual teachers have increasingly come to stress a bicultural focus as compared to the English-dominant school training of the past.

Los Angeles has become a mixing bowl of different races and nationalities. A 700-unit black housing development south of Watts bears the name Ujima Community Development. During the decade of the 1970s plans to rebuild "Little Tokyo" were also put forth. That neighborhood, now a hundred years old, boasts a new hotel, the Otani. This and other tourist attractions have helped to arrest and sometimes reverse urban blight. Such attractions also call attention to the industriousness and innovation of the city's ethnic groups.

A good many writers have portrayed the Japanese struggle to overcome the wartime stereotypes of treacherous subhumans capable of great cruelty and inhumanity. White prejudice and suspicion grew during the interwar period. Once World War II broke out, the Japanese community suffered the indignity of relocation in concentration camps—from the bleachers under the Santa Anita Racetrack's grandstands to distant Tule Lake. After the war the Japanese, having been brusquely dispersed, sought to accommodate themselves to the dominant society by becoming model citizens. They earned a reputation for hard work and economic success. The role of the Japanese gardener and nurseryman became a virtual cliché. Eventually, however, the Nisei, or members of the second-generation born in the United States, developed mixed feelings toward the ethnic constraints their parents placed upon them. Recently they have been seeking to identify themselves as a distinct generation that is better educated and less needful of public or family approval.

For the Japanese (and such other nationalities as the Italians) all these shifts in public and private feeling have been reflected in their movement out of traditional housing centers. Within Los Angeles there remain only the enclaves of the older centers—for example, the area along Sawtelle Boulevard north of Olympic and south of Wilshire, where an active remnant of the Japanese plant nursery trade continues to thrive. The newer Asian generations have settled in the Hollywood-Wilshire district, on the west side, and in Monterey Park, Alhambra, and the central-city areas. In 1981 the Japanese-American population of Los Angeles was estimated to be 110,000.

The local Japanese community has produced a major talent, the architectural planner Isamu Noguchi. He has designed a one-acre plaza as the focal point for a Japanese American Cultural Center, to be located between Second and Third on San Pedro Street. Noguchi is called by some critics the world's most important living sculptor. His projects are to be found from Tel Aviv to Hiroshima, with concentrations in major cities of the United States. Asked how he felt about doing a project where he was born (in 1904), he replied: "L.A is like a place you have up your sleeve. It used to be where people retired. I am not retiring. I am just passing through here." [6]

Early in 1981 Arata Isozaki, yet another Japanese, was chosen to design a new $16 million Museum of Contemporary Art. His imaginative architectural productions feature the combining of cylinders, rectangles, boxes, prisms, and undulating planes. An influential member of the board planning Los Angeles's newest museum is Seiji Tsutsumi, an international businessman, novelist, and poet who also heads a consortium of over a hundred companies and several research institutes.

Recently the arrival of immigrants from different areas of the world has diversified the city's cultural mix. Among regions represented are Korea, Vietnam, Hong Kong, and the west coast Latin American countries, especially Ecuador and Chile. The transition of Los Angeles into a conglomeration of these new races and nationalities has featured emergence of an Asian middle class. Asians and Pacific Islanders have the lowest school drop-out rate and the highest median income, as compared with blacks and Latinos. The employment rate among Asians is also high and their welfare rate low. They form the city's newest middle class.

By 1980 there were 65,000 Koreans in Los Angeles, or one percent of the metropolitan area's population. Living near Vermont and Olympic boulevards, they constitute the largest settlement of Koreans outside Korea. Following in the footsteps of the Chinese and Japanese, many have become economically successful. Today the merchants of "Koreatown" own an agglomeration of over two hundred commercial properties along Olympic Boulevard and Eighth Street. They have dramatically changed the appearance of a formerly WASP neighborhood.

The Jews were among the first of the city's minorities to stake out a geographical area which reflects their tastes and interests. At first they lived in Boyle Heights and in the central city, but now they have scattered to the west side and into the San Fernando Valley, though many have congregated in the Fairfax district where Old World flavor lingers on. As one walks down the streets, Yiddish, Hebrew, and Russian can be heard. It is also one of the few areas of the city where one meets newly arrived immigrants from Russia and Israel.[7]

To a lesser extent have the Italians and French retained their civic identity. In recent years Italian priests of the Salesian order have established a Casa Italiana, located on the grounds of St. Peter's Catholic Church on North Broadway. This area, now a center of Chinese activity, once teemed with Italian grocery stores, restaurants, an ethnic newspaper, and other small businesses. The French Hospital in the center of "Chinatown" is another remnant that reflects the shift in population patterns. Long forgotten is the 1871 massacre of nineteen Chinese. Block after block of the central city now belongs to them.[8]

After World War I, Greeks, Armenians, Serbs, and Croatians fled Europe in droves. More than a hundred thousand Armenians are spread throughout the Los Angeles region, with concentrations in Pasadena, Glendale, and Montebello. The Greeks settled heavily in Boyle Heights and Gardena. They built their own cathedral as a place of worship with the aid of the movie mogul Spyros Skouras. The Serbs tended to settle in Baldwin Park and Monterey Park as well as in the San Gabriel Valley, while the Croats favored San Pedro and the area north of the civic center where they have their church, St. Anthony's. Formerly some of its oldest parishioners were fishermen from the Dalmatian coastline of Yugoslavia.

Other nationalities include the Germans (some 20,000 in Los Angeles County), Russians (10,000), Lithuanians (5,000), and more recently Iranians who have brought both money and the Farsi tongue to already affluent Beverly Hills.

By 1980 it could be said that if you lived anywhere in Los Angeles County, you were a member of a minority group. This became true even if you were an Anglo, for no national or racial group could claim fifty percent of the population. Here is one estimate of the county's present composition:

Anglo	3.4 million	46%
Hispanic	2.5 million	34%
Black	1 million	13%
Asian	400,000	5%
Other non-white	140,00	2%

If a trend set during the last decade continues, Hispanics will no longer be a minority group. According to one estimate they will account for over half of the county's population in one more decade. During the period 1970–1980 there was a pronounced reversal of the "Anglo" population count:

	Increase (or decrease) 1970–1980
Total population	+400,000
Anglo	−1.3 million
Hispanic	+1.2 million
Black and other non-white	+500,000

As for the city, in 1980 a quarter of its population consisted of persons eighteen years old or younger. But only 39.7 percent of these youths were "Anglos," followed by 23.2 percent Hispanics and 22.4 percent blacks. As is obvious, more than 50 percent of the aggregate population of Los Angeles comprises these minority members, in addition to Asians.[9] There are other seldom mentioned groups as well. More Samoans live in southern California than on the islands from which they came. Los

Angeles is also said to have more American Indians than any other city in the United States, partly the result of the federal government's relocation programs.

The most aggrieved of all these minorities are the blacks and Chicanos. Their struggle to achieve equality of opportunity continues to be reflected in the busing of minority children from disadvantaged areas into WASP neighborhoods and the busing of whites into minority centers. Court-ordered, this solution has produced less than satisfactory results. While a measure of school desegregation has been achieved, dissatisfaction of both minority parents and those from more affluent neighborhoods continues. Legal wrangles lasting for years have ensued. The Los Angeles school board has been repeatedly charged with foot-dragging.

The lengthy controversy over the busing of minority children, in order to achieve integration, was bound to end up in the courts. In June 1976 the California Supreme Court ruled against the Los Angeles school board in a thirteen-year-old desegregation case and ordered the board to take "reasonably feasible" steps to reduce segregation. Superior Court Judge Paul Egly then began hearings on the board's proposals to integrate the Los Angeles public schools. He managed to keep pressure on the school board for almost five years. Meanwhile, sentiment against court-ordered desegregation began to mount. Public criticism of "forced busing" grew. So did accelerated flight of white students to the suburbs.

Even private and church-affiliated schools felt the pressure of the federal government over segregation. At one point the Internal Revenue Service threatened that schools which did not accept pupils of all racial and ethnic backgrounds would lose their tax-exempt status. Thus, federal as well as state power lay behind the emotional busing issue. Coverage by the media of the busing controversy was seldom neutral. Blacks too joined in criticizing the busing of their children to distant schools.

Finally, early in 1981, the anti-busing forces achieved significant legislative and court victories. These decisions virtually reversed Judge Egly's previous pro-busing mandates. As a result, the school board began the dismantling of its elaborate busing network.

Delays in implementing court integration mandates also in-furiated those advocates of busing who are anxious to overcome segregated housing patterns. Furthermore, anti–fair housing forces have also made repeated attempts to repeal ordinances and legislation designed to remedy segregation. The battles over segregation are reflected in the drop of Caucasian school enrollment. By 1972 minority enrollment in the Los Angeles public schools had reached 39.8 percent. Caucasian enrollment during the previous five years had declined by 12 percent. In 1980 only 27 percent of the children in the city schools were Caucasians.

Demographers predict that by 1984 Latinos will constitute a third of the general Los Angeles population. Although Asians in 1980 were only seven percent of the population, they too are quickly expected to exceed that percentage.[10] The internation-alization of Los Angeles is a phenomenon that even sociologists and professional historians did not properly anticipate. It is now well under way.

The myth that foreigners would, somehow, all become inte-grated into one bland nationality was bound to give way to the opposite—today's "ethnic pluralism." We all wish to know our roots, a process that means remaining faithful to origins rather than giving way to a perverted "melting pot" imagery. At Los Angeles, ethnicity has reclaimed its rightful place in the history of the city.

CHAPTER TEN

The
Tomorrow
City

L ONG AGO demographers foresaw that Los Angeles would become a speeded-up prototype of that urbanization which today threatens to engulf the major cities of the world. This urban sprawl, with its satellite residential suburbs, has accompanied a massive shift from an agricultural to an industrial society. Following World War I, a period of "thirty explosive years" saw the emergence of hundreds of new industrial plants. A construction boom followed that featured the appearance of hundreds of housing tracts.[1]

An updated epithet about Los Angeles no longer describes it jokingly as a group of suburbs in search of a city but now as a city connected by concrete and smog. Because mobility is its central hallmark, Los Angeles depends on the automobile as does no other metropolis. As it struggles to accommodate three million autos, smog has become one of its most serious problems. This noxious air pollution, which stems from increasing industrialization and high automobile density, forced Los Angeles in the early 1950s to organize a County Air Pollution Control District, which has spent millions of dollars trying to rid the city of eye-irritating fumes.

The charge has been made that Los Angeles has been losing the battle to control smog. Population growth cancels out air-control measures, but politicians seem reluctant to combat industry and housing developers. Furthermore, three levels of government—federal, state, and district—help to determine how Los Angeles conducts its war on smog. Ironically, local authority seems the weakest and least determined unit of government, whereas state and federal agencies have tended to keep the pressure up to control the filthiest and most toxic air in the world. But interagency squabbles as well as lawsuits and the calling of names have produced their own bureaucratic pollution. Only eighty-six field inspectors (during 1981) monitored between sixty and eighty thousand pollution sources. There has been heavy reliance upon industry to comply voluntarily with pollution regulations. According to an Air Quality Management Plan, there should be clean air in the Los Angeles basin by 1987; but such promises have been made before. They regularly occur in the speeches of politicians who do the least to enforce compliance with smog-control regulations.

Had Los Angeles maintained its original rapid transit system, the problem of pollution would surely have taken a different turn. But gone are the "Big Red Cars" of the Pacific Electric Railway, the best public transport system Los Angeles has ever known. Now the city is sometimes referred to as "four thousand acres of parking lots." Lewis Mumford once estimated that two-thirds of its central area is occupied by facilities devoted to automobiles: garages, service stations, and streets. Despite all this emphasis upon autos, an intricately designed freeway system has not solved worsening transport problems. Meanwhile, debates about subways versus monorails for rapid transit remain interminable.

During the late 1950s the Los Angeles area grew by as many as 240,000 persons per year. There were days when a thousand permanent new residents arrived. This caused school authorities to open at least one new school per week in order to keep pace with population growth. At the end of World War II, Los Angeles was not flooded with aging pensioners, as had been predicted, but by youthful ex-servicemen who formed family households.

With diminishing agricultural lands available for leapfrogging housing tracts, a shift from single-family homes to apartments increased. The skyline became filled with tall buildings. A new

Los Angeles skyline, 1976. (*Courtesy Victor R. Plukas.*)

"highrise" style of architecture—which featured glass and light-weight metal buildings—gradually converted downtown Los Angeles and the Wilshire district into an area of multistoried apartments and office buildings. From the 1950s onward recon-struction of the central civic area radically altered the city's downtown configuration. Dozens of new tall buildings arose around a central mall and civic center. Typical was the redevel-opment with federal aid of Bunker Hill, a blighted slum zone. This rejuvenation of its central core increased the economic health and physical attraction of Los Angeles, but displaced old and indigent residents who lived in the area.

The 1960 census showed that Los Angeles, with a population of 2,479,015, was the only major American city that had not lost residents to its suburbs in the decade preceding. This was partly due to incorporation of those areas into the city. Los Angeles County, with a population count of 6,038,771 persons, was, in 1960, the most populous county in the United States. Since then growth has slowed markedly. Indeed, from 1965 onward a considerable out-migration occurred. Yet, by 1970, county population stood at 7,032,000. The out-migration fig-

ures have been moderated by significant gains in the number of
births. This increase, in turn, has been partly due to the high
birth rates of the Hispanic population. The county, thus, has
registered net increases of 40,000 per year since 1974 (when
the county experienced its first population drop in 123 years).
By 1980, county population stood at 7,130,000, a figure that
reflects a relatively slow rate of growth. The county acts as a
"gateway" through which new residents pass before settling
permanently elsewhere. Most such persons later move to
Orange, San Bernardino, Ventura, Riverside, and San Diego
counties.

By 1980 city population reached 2,966,763, up 154,962 or
5.5 percent from the year 1970. Among the nation's six cities
with more than one million population, only two—Houston
and Los Angeles—registered increases between 1970 and 1980.
At Los Angeles the latest count—almost 3 million inhabitants—
indicates that it will soon replace Chicago as the second largest
city in the United States.

For much of the last century it was central Los Angeles
proper that grew in population. The 1980 census, however,
indicated that the city's suburbs and exurbs had gained in population at a faster rate than the center city. In the previous decade
Los Angeles County had also grown by a scant 5.3 percent,
ranking fifty-third among the state's fifty-eight counties in rate
of growth. However, it is still the state's largest county by far. It
gained nearly four hundred thousand people from 1970 to

Population Projections

COUNTY	1985	2000
Alameda	1,194,800	1,358,100
Los Angeles	7,122,900	7,850,400
Orange	2,233,900	2,810,600
San Diego	2,022,400	2,654,100
San Francisco	653,500	656,600
Santa Clara	1,487,800	1,804,900
The State	24,363,000	29,277,000

SOURCE: Population Research Unit of the Department of Finance, Sacramento.

1980, more than the total of the sixteen fastest-growing counties combined.

The 1970 census found that slightly more than one in three people in California lived in Los Angeles County. As a result of the county's slower growth rate in the '70s, slightly fewer than one in three Californians now live in Los Angeles County. Population growth, however, was uneven. In the last decade some cities in Los Angeles County actually lost population. These included Artesia, Torrance, El Segundo, Downey, and the two "golden ghettoes," San Marino and Beverly Hills. The latter communities seemed to reflect a trend toward fewer children in affluent homes. Some families simply did not replicate themselves. In such inner-cities as Hollywood and Silver Lake, many single-unit homes were converted to multiple-unit homes with a resulting increase in population.

The fastest-growing city in Los Angeles County was Cerritos, which increased by nearly 232 percent during the decade. Cerritos is on the edge of the county, halfway between downtown Los Angeles and Irvine. In 1967, Dairy Valley became Cerritos—a name identified with its community college and originating from land-grant days when the region was part of Rancho Los Cerritos. As recently as 1968, Cerritos had only 4,373 people. Growing rapidly into a modern city, it had 37,000 people by 1972. A vigorous government-aided redevelopment program was partly responsible for this unusual growth. Cerritos dairymen ended up operating gasoline stations. Vacant former dairylands were much more attractive for redevelopment than decaying central-city properties. Until recently such farm-to-city "growth" would have been unhesitatingly applauded. There was plenty of agricultural land available, even in Los Angeles County, to produce the crops which the city needed. What has happened to Cerritos in the last few years, however, illustrates how much valuable farm land is being lost annually to developers.

Despite recession conditions, by 1980 Los Angeles led the state's fifty-eight counties in housing construction volume. A trend toward luxury condominiums is exemplified by the numerous highrise buildings along Wilshire Boulevard between Westwood and Beverly Hills. Supplementing single- and multi-family dwellings are mobile homes, which account for about

four percent of southern California's housing stock. The demand for housing and commercial facilities continues to out-
pace supply, partly due to the high interest rates of the 1980s.
Thus, there is an increasing trend toward smaller homes on
smaller lots, more condominiums and townhouses, more manufactured housing and mobile homes, and toward inclusionary
and government-subsidized housing for low- and moderate-
income persons.

The city's actual marketing area potentially covers five counties containing some eleven million persons. The buying power
of Los Angeles is estimated as exceeding the combined total of
Houston, Cleveland, Baltimore, Miami, and Denver. Its retail
sales are currently greater than those of New York, Chicago,
Philadelphia, or Detroit. Over ten million tourists come to the
city each year. Los Angeles has the highest automobile-to-
people ratio of any city in the world. More stock and mutual-
fund shareholders live in L.A. than in any other United States
city. If Los Angeles were a separate country, its gross product
would rank ahead of all but fifteen nations. These achievements
have contributed to a boosterish mentality, but one not quite so
blatant as that ascribed to residents of Texas.

Prodigal in its consumption of material goods, Los Angeles
has, like Dallas, depleted its once rich supply of oil. In the 1920s
a sizable percentage of the world's oil was produced in the L.A.
basin. Water, too, remains a scarce resource. Today an average
urban family of four uses approximately an acre-foot of water
(325,851 gallons) per year. This is nearly enough to cover a
football field with one foot of water. It takes another 4,500
gallons of water to grow the food for one person for one day. If
one orders a hamburger with french fries and a soft drink at a
fast-food restaurant, 1,472 gallons of water have been used by
farmers to produce the meat, lettuce, grain, tomato, potato, and
sugar contained in that serving. The use of water for refrigera-
tion and industrial purposes is also massive.[2]

Three-fourths of California's rain normally falls in the northern third of the state. Unfortunately, while the cost of developing additional water supplies is escalating, the average household's rate of water consumption is relatively insensitive to price
increases. The demand for water at Los Angeles has nearly

always exceeded available supplies. In 1913, when William Mulholland brought in water from the Owens Basin some 230 miles distant, many Angelenos believed that their population would never surpass two hundred thousand persons. Within the next decade the city quadrupled in size. Today millions of Los Angeles residents rely upon water from Mono Lake and the Colorado River, and from the California Aqueduct, which draws it from the Feather River and beyond.

Up north a massive plant near Tracy pumps the water uphill toward Bakersfield in Kern County. There it is repumped over the Tehachapi range. All this effort involves moving the water higher than the highest falls in North America. The Castaic and Perris reservoirs then store it for later use by the Metropolitan Water District of Southern California (MWD). Electricity is generated along the route but much oil-energy must be expended to keep the water flowing into the city.

The MWD is a major force in state water development, dictating water policy not only within Los Angeles but for cities in six counties. This is partly because the city's taxpayers have contributed vast amounts to the state water project's development. The MWD wholesales surplus water to users outside Los Angeles.

As water resources have grown scarcer in recent years, the MWD has pressed Spanish riparian legal claims that remain questionable. In a massive lawsuit that lasted for some years, advocates of Los Angeles invoked an alleged "prior and paramount pueblo water right." Yet it was the clear policy of Spain and Mexico to share the waters among all the inhabitants of a territory, including the Indians. This self-serving assertion of supremacy added to the reputation of the city as a voracious symbolic sponge. The surrounding communities of Pasadena, Glendale, Burbank, and San Fernando have had to curtail their drilling of subsurface water within the Los Angeles basin as a result of repeated legal action against all such users, including private businesses.

As we have seen, Angelenos have been prodigal in their use of water and oil resources. Until quite recently they also hardly seemed interested in conserving their material history and its residual landmarks. Long before renovation of Carroll Street became fashionable, Los Angeles physically repudiated its past.

Historic buildings of significance were regularly torn down to create parking lots or shopping centers. The rationale featured overuse of the word "progress." In 1969 Bunker Hill's two remaining nineteenth-century mansions, the "Castle" and the "Salt Box," were temporarily salvaged and transported to another site, only to be destroyed by fires set by vandals. In their place came an "urban renewal" in which the hill's natural contours and profile were reshaped. Now air-conditioned, tall buildings replace the Victorian wooden houses once so familiar. It was as though the city enshrined mechanized growth over tradition. About this phenomenon one commentator wrote that "L.A. is bound up with technology like no other city in history, and technology has a will of its own." [3]

A polite way to describe the senseless demolition of its past is to call Los Angeles a center of architectural experimentation, of "starting over." But since the 1920s, when refreshment stands were built to resemble hot dogs, critics have sensed a zaniness without roots in the emergence of a city. Not all local construction, of course, has been tasteless; but much of it is scarcely for the ages. Today it is merely amusing that brash developers in 1936 would have called a smallish shopping mall "The Crossroads of the World." Also, the proliferation of the "streamline moderne" architecture of the 1930s has not held up well. To outsiders the neon and plastic landscape now seems eclectic, confounding, and contradictory.

Architect Cliff May, the best-known proponent of the split-level ranch house ("splanch"), discovered an insatiable residential market, as did swimming-pool contractors (before the 1970s energy crunch). For Los Angeles had come to possess a higher proportion of privately owned family dwellings than any other large city—perhaps in the entire world. Their owners, furthermore, were fond of moving, usually upgrading their status with each change of address. The highrises that increasingly flanked the city's major arteries employed what came to be called "high tech" features. In order to increase productivity, Los Angeles became a center of modular assembly-line buildings. How treasured will these seem in decades to come? [4]

Future critics may relate the brainless sprawl with which Los Angeles became afflicted to the saddest aspect of the city's recent development—its failure to plan grandly or carefully for the future. The lack of a modern transportation system is the most direct casualty of a general lack of both leadership and public consensus. More accurately, what has occurred has discouraged local officials, who have seen plan after plan and bond issue after bond issue go down to defeat.

In 1970 the mayor's office, for example, launched a "blueprint for development into the year 2000," which envisioned a planning concept for the future that would tie together forty-seven of the city's urban centers. The plan would have allowed Los Angeles to retain its single-family life style while restructuring existing highrise residential and business zones. The plan also sought to reverse urban deterioration and to create a unified city. But the problem of every Los Angeles mayor in modern times has been to achieve a consensus among conflicting interests, all intent upon keeping taxes low. Hence, this well-inspired concept was again derailed by an ambivalent electorate.[5] There is a continuing paradox between the city's desire to grow in a modern way and its handling of change.

Historically, also, as we have already noted, the mayors of Los Angeles have been burdened by a city charter that weakens their discretionary powers. Amalgamation of basic city functions, thus, remains a pious hope mouthed at press conferences and for newspaper releases. The heads of commissions and departments—police, water and power, airport, and harbor—have been the true chiefs of city government. The city council has exerted only limited control over department heads once they were appointed. As with other cities, costly and unnecessary layers of government have proliferated. Among these is a seemingly unmanageable Department of Public Works. Other departments and commissions have also proven to be unresponsive, unnecessary, and wasteful. Only in recent years have revisions of the charter made possible more centralized control by the mayor's office, yet the real control remains largely in the hands of others.

Los Angeles has refused to abandon addiction to the automobile, despite the congestion, noise, and noxious fumes which it causes. The first page-one story on smog appeared in the *Los Angeles Times* on July 27, 1943. It was headlined as follows: "City Hunting for Source of Gas Attack." A subtitle read: "Thousands Left with Sore Eyes and Throats by Irritating

Fumes." From that time a frustrating debate continues on the origins of smog: "Yesterday's annoyance was at least the fourth such attack of recent days, and by far the worst. The city health department says the fumes are emanating from a new synthetic rubber plant." The Kaiser steel mill at Fontana was also blamed for the eye irritation, as were backyard incinerators, which were eventually banned after a long debate about the right of citizens to dispose of their garbage as they saw fit. Expert advice was sought from the California Institute of Technology as to the origins of smog, as though such opinion would quickly solve the problem. New layers of government, including the Air Pollution Control District, were added to the bureaucracy. Failure after failure occurred in controlling noxious emissions. The smog problem seemed to worsen as each year passed. Fascination with the freedom of automobile travel caused massive resistance against fitting vehicles with catalytic converters. In-

Mayors of Los Angeles

1850 Alpheus P. Hodges	1888 John Bryson
1851 Benjamin D. Wilson	1889 Henry T. Hazard
1852 John G. Nichols	1892 Thomas E. Rowan
1853 Antonio F. Coronel	1894 Frank Rader
1854 Stephen C. Foster	1896 Meredith P. Snyder
1855 Thomas Foster	1898 Fred Eaton
1856 Stephen C. Foster	1900 Meredith P. Snyder
John G. Nichols	1904 Owen C. McAleer
1859 Damien Marchessault	1906 Arthur C. Harper
1860 Henry Mellus	1909 William D. Stephens
1861 Damien Marchessault	George Alexander
1865 Jose Mascarel	1913 Henry R. Rose
1866 Cristobal Aguilar	1915 Charles E. Sebastian
1868 Joel H. Turner	1916 Frederick T. Woodman
1871 Cristobal Aguilar	1919 Meredith P. Snyder
1872 James R. Toberman	1921 George E. Cryer
1874 Prudent Beaudry	1929 John C. Porter
1876 Frederick A. MacDougall	1933 Frank L. Shaw
1878 James R. Toberman	1938 Fletcher Bowron
1882 Cameron E. Thom	1953 Norris Poulson
1884 Edward F. Spence	1961 Sam Yorty
1884 William H. Workman	1973 Thomas Bradley

deed, reluctance to blame the auto continues into the present.

Repeatedly voters refused to cooperate as to alternative transit. Reflecting this selfish myopia were three elections—1968, 1974, and 1976—in which voters turned down multimillion-dollar transit proposals. Every time such plans were seriously revived, federal money was not available, or some other roadblock, such as the disparateness of the local geography, was put forth as an excuse not to proceed with building a rapid transit system. One result was to remain a car-dependent community with a rickety transportation base.

Any discussion of transportation in Los Angeles must not exclude the powerful influence of the auto lobby. Its persuasive spokesman for three-quarters of a century has been the Automobile Club of Southern California. Headquartered within the city since 1900, this organization is partially responsible for its decentralization and for the growth of its suburbs. Major oil companies and auto dealers, too, have discouraged rapid transit. These critics still continue to charge that public transportation systems could not survive densities of four to six families per acre without some form of subsidy. Meanwhile, each year's delay in funding a rapid-transit system has led construction costs to grow astronomically because of inflation.

In 1968, if only five percent more voters had supported it, the city could have begun construction of a rapid-transit system. Finally, in 1980, the electorate did approve a watered-down version of previous transit proposals, with virtually no leadership by the mayor or other public officials. This measure (mostly designed to expand existing bus lines and to reduce fares) also called for creation of a 160-mile county-wide rail network. As the measure, however, was passed without a two-thirds majority (receiving only 54 percent of the vote), the entire package became subject to legal challenges in the courts. Furthermore, as other cities across the country received federal subsidies to build or to revive old transportation systems, Los Angeles was stymied by demands for countless annual surveys and feasibility studies.

Meanwhile, both state and federal funding support dried up as inflation diluted the tax base. These negative factors occurred during the crucial bicentennial year, 1981, when plans seemed to be shaping up, finally, for construction of two key projects. These were a downtown "people mover" to cover the route from the convention center to the Union Station. The second was the long-discussed "Wilshire corridor" subway line. Los Angeles was to pay heavily, and quite literally, for its indecision and poor leadership. Stringent governmental budget cuts, national, state, and local, threaten to sideline both projects. Without outside subsidies, mass transit seems destined to wallow in the quagmire which the voters themselves have sanctioned.

A S TIME PASSED, Los Angeles began to resemble a country by itself rather than any other city. This postindustrial sun-belt metropolis stands outside the national urban pattern, according to most specialists. Criticism of it has been both justified and irresponsible. The public had gradually developed a fantasy-mentality that defied description but was commercially profitable. Instant illusions of both antiquity and futurism were available to tourists and residents alike. For example, at the Los Angeles harbor promoters built an entire New England fishing village, "Ports of Call," which flourished. Knott's Berry Farm, once noted for its berry pies and fried chicken, installed vintage railroad locomotives, an 1849 gold mine, and a western street setting that rivaled the best movie set. Disneyland not only provided visitors with a "magic kingdom," its operators also installed a Matterhorn Alpine peak, a Mississippi River steamboat, and one of the first monorail lines in the country. Even Premier Nikita Khrushchev of the Soviet Union wanted to visit Walt Disney's make-believe "lands."

Critics and admirers alike find it as difficult to discern a unifying conceptual center in Los Angeles as to identify a single weather pattern. Comedian Bob Hope (who enriched himself via Los Angeles real estate) once quipped that it is the only place on earth where one can experience fire, flood, and an earthquake on the same day. The "cemetery culture," lampooned by Aldous Huxley and Evelyn Waugh, does not much help us to define the Los Angeles ethos. Neither does Forest Lawn cemetery's reproduction of world-famous art, or the plasticized Brown Derby restaurant, or car washes festooned with Victorian lamps—or the other schlock architectural excesses that litter the city. Out of all this confusion, and the search for centrality, have emerged such updated epithets as the "incredible" city, the "nowhere" city, "slurburbia," and latterly, the "improbable" city.[6]

Perhaps L.A. has given newcomers a greater opportunity to act out character disorders and anxieties than other communities, but this is conjecture. If eccentricity and a "kinky" life style remain endemic, it would be more fruitful to probe the reasons for the city's perpetuation of these characteristics than to foster labels upon it. Yet one detects a tendency (even by the most substantial of its past interpreters) simply to avoid discussion of unpleasant social realities. One of these is crime. With relatively little public notice, juvenile gangs grew steadily from the 1960s onward until they today pose a major public menace. In 1980 the toll of gang murders in Los Angeles County was estimated at over 300 deaths. Allegedly, one stands a greater chance of dying by homicide than in an auto accident. Here and elsewhere crime has reached epidemic proportions. So has the police "kill rate," and there are repeated charges of police brutality, especially toward minority groups.

A few statistics are in order. Every fourteen hours one homicide occurs within the city of Los Angeles. The homicide rate is 23.9 for each 100,000 residents. Seven reported rapes take place every day as do 539 reported thefts. Not all thefts or rapes, of course, are reported. The theft toll has risen to 7,207 per 100,000 inhabitants.

As for county crime statistics, in 1980 Sheriff Peter Pitchess revealed that during the last twenty years its homicide rate had increased by a startling 426 percent. He predicted that total murders would exceed by nearly a thousand the 1,557 killings of 1979.

In the city itself, there were 804 criminal homicides that year. By 1980 the Los Angeles city murder count had risen to 1,021, making it the bloodiest year in its history. This 27 percent jump in the murder rate pushed the city ahead of Chicago as the second most murderous metropolis in America. That distinction belonged to New York, where 1,737 murders occurred during 1980. Additionally, the 1980 figures show increases in all seven

major crime categories, with 297,443 reported offenses that
year. Police Chief Daryl F. Gates has revealed that the most
significant increases were recorded in "violent crimes," the sort
that instill the most fear in the community. The year 1980 also
saw a 25.5 percent increase in city robberies and a 15.8 percent
growth in the number of burglaries over the year before. Aggra-
vated assaults, too, climbed from 20,332 in 1979 to 21,484
reported in 1980, a 5.7 percent increase.[7]

The avoidance of such harsh realities has led Angelenos to
focus upon pleasantries that sometimes appear superficial and
synthetic. Perhaps symbolic of the city's continuing lotus-land
reputation is the Triforium, a relatively recent (1978) accretion
built in its civic center. Instead of constructing a subway station
or two, repeatedly sidelined, the city boasts this most unusual
gadget—located in its high tower and lighted at night. This
expensive monstrosity also consists of a musical instrument
electronically activated by glass tubes—in short, a trinket instead of a tool.

Is there an immaturity about Los Angeles that encourages the
ephemeral? Does the local public tend to value amusement
over civic substance? Richard Lillard has described southern
California as speeding "from one brilliant improvisation to another, valuing means, neglecting ends." He sees the sun as
never rising or setting "twice on the same landscape," the city
having become "a triumph of American genius and greed."[8]

After two hundred years, the time has surely come for the
pursuit of a more solid destiny.[9] Los Angeles County, now with
a population in excess of seven million, has more people than
forty sovereign nations and more automobiles than any foreign
nation. Only four entire American states surpass Los Angeles
County's auto registrations. A publication of a local bank bears
the title *The Sixty Mile Circle*. This it describes as an arc within
sixty miles of downtown Los Angeles, including Orange County
and most of Riverside, San Bernardino, and Ventura counties.
Population within this sixty-mile circle totals eleven million persons—the second-largest concentration of people, business,
and industry in the United States. The area also accounts for
nearly half the economy of California.

Angelenos, as we have seen, sometimes choose private satisfactions over public needs—the family auto has come before a balanced transport system. Housing tracts took precedence over planned communities. There have been exceptions, of course, but it is as though a society first wished to make up for the material shortages of the Depression and later for deprivations during World War II. Then the pursuit of materialistic gain led to environmental shabbiness, to housing and public buildings that began to fall apart shortly after they were built. Yet architectural experimentation has been a local constant for decades—from the relatively simple bungalows built nearly two-thirds of a century ago by the Green brothers to the grandiosity of today's Century City.

Los Angeles remains a city of firsts. One senses the urge to create something new, as though the past were an enemy. Boosters and thoughtful residents alike have taken pride in this characteristic. While some regret that political leadership is not brighter, local citizens supported the first recall election in the nation and provided the first public defender. They have sponsored healthy bits of city planning, too, including the first hillside grading ordinance. Sporadic efforts toward saving the environment resulted in the first zoning regulations to separate industrial from residential areas. This has aided the regulation of industrial smoke pollution. The Arroyo Seco Freeway was one of the first in the entire country, its construction supported, of course, by more than city revenues. Applied science and scholarship on a mass scale have generally flourished in the region, although standards for the latter could be higher. Foot-dragging has unfortunately characterized local compliance with national integration laws—this despite the fact that the first major black riot in the country occurred in the suburb of Watts.

There is growing concern about the limits of frenzied growth. Polluted air, indeed, may simply be a symptom of an overburdened environment. There is evidence that the ecosystem of the Los Angeles basin has been oversaturated with housing projects, freeways, business developments (legitimate and honkytonk), of which smog is both by-product and symbol.

The city, however, still vacillates between the historic antitheses of being bigger yet better at the same time. Although critics see Los Angeles as gradually emerging from a corridor of mediocrity, they yearn for that depth of culture which produced an Athens or a Rome. The boosterism of earlier times seems to have moderated. Although coyotes still abound in the surrounding hills, more than a modest beginning has been made toward the creation of a center of vitality among the palm trees. Los Angeles is no longer the socially arid, oversold half-city of the interwar era. Smog, the movies, oil, freeways, television, the air and missile industry have all played a part in leading yesterday's cow town into modernity. Other cultural contributors have included scholars, artists, and retired leaders of other communities who have moved to the sun-belt cities of the Southwest. The latter support with their wealth local colleges and universities, concerts, gourmet restaurants, and plays, as well as other public events. So do corporations, for whom Los Angeles has become a headquarters city. Decisions about grants to the arts can be made on the spot. Today, only New York City launches more legitimate stage productions each year than Los Angeles. Scientists and literary folk, too, seem concerned about education and the arts in a wholly new way. These changes in attitude have accelerated since the middle 1950s, and they have helped to overcome the city's perversity and lack of commonly held cultural values. Critics would nevertheless continue to charge that an innocent confusion persists about the true nature of quality in the life of this particular society.

The city's ultimate form, of course, remains uncertain. It is still unfinished, endlessly changing, restless, relying heavily upon a technological base for its future development. Despite its turbulence, greediness, and wayward standards, there are those who are optimistic about that future—as though Los Angeles were a dynamic paradise, even Shangri-la. Indeed, such folk may criticize endlessly but would live in no other place on earth.

NOTES

CHAPTER ONE

1. W. W. Robinson gathered up these epithets in *What They Say about the Angels* (Pasadena: Val Trefz Press, 1942). See also Jack Smith, "The Knock Knock Game," *Los Angeles Times,* June 22, 1978, and "Sierra Club Chief Calls L.A. Mistake, An Utter Disaster," ibid., August 28, 1970.

2. As a result, Los Angeles has grown from an area of 28.01 square miles in 1850 to 464 square miles (1202 square kilometers) in 1980. New York City's land area is only 320 square miles. The Los Angeles County area is 4,083 square miles.

CHAPTER TWO

1. See George Harwood Phillips, "Indians in Los Angeles, 1781–1875: Economic Integration, Social Disintegration," *Pacific Historical Review,* XLIX (August 1980), 428; and Bernice Eastman Johnston, *California's Gabrielino Indians* (Los Angeles: Southwest Museum, 1962), the only book-length study of these natives.

2. Good summary translations of the original documents about the founding of Los Angeles are printed in Historical Society of Southern California, *Annual Publications* XV (Los Angeles: 1931). This volume commemorated the 150th anniversary of the city. Another basic source is Thomas Workman Temple, Jr., "Se Fundaron un Pueblo de Españoles," *ibid.,* 69–98.

3. See the chapter entitled "Abel Stearns: The Personification of an Age," in Robert G. Cleland, *The Cattle on a Thousand Hills* (3rd ed., San Marino: Huntington Library, 1951), 184–207; see also William W. Clary, *History of the Law Firm of O'Melveny & Myers, 1885–1965* (Los Angeles: privately printed, 1966), 207–215.

CHAPTER THREE

1. See George R. Brooks, ed., *The Southwest Expeditions of Jedediah S. Smith* (Glendale: A. H. Clark, 1977).

2. *The Personal Narrative of James O. Pattie of Kentucky* (Cincinnati: 1831), reprinted in Reuben Gold Thwaites, ed., *Early Western Travels*

(Cleveland: Arthur H. Clark, 1905), XVIII, 278. Pattie's exploits are engagingly recounted in Robert G. Cleland, *This Reckless Breed of Men* (New York: Knopf, 1950), 159–208.

3. Consult Iris Wilson, *William Wolfskill, 1798–1866: Frontier Trapper to California Ranchero* (Glendale: Arthur H. Clark, 1965).

4. Details are in Werner H. Marti, *Messenger of Destiny* (San Francisco: John Howell Books, 1960).

5. The situation is nicely described in Dwight L. Clarke, *Stephen Watts Kearny, Soldier of the West* (Norman: University of Oklahoma Press, 1961).

6. Andrew F. Rolle, "New Flag over Fort Moore," *Westways*, XLVIII (Sept. 1956), 4–5.

7. Quoted in Philip Tyson, *Geology and Industrial Resources of California* (Baltimore: W. Minifie & Co., 1851), 17.

CHAPTER FOUR

1. Roscoe P. and Margaret B. Conkling, *The Butterfield Overland Mail* (3 vols., Glendale: Arthur H. Clark, 1947) is useful.

2. On Baldwin, see C. B. Glasscock, *Lucky Baldwin* (Indianapolis: Bobbs-Merrill, 1933). Regarding Reid, see Susanna Bryant Dakin, *A Scotch Paisano* (Berkeley: University of California Press, 1939).

3. The camels are described in Lewis B. Lesley, *Uncle Sam's Camels* (Cambridge, Mass.: Harvard University Press, 1929), and in Harlan Fowler, *Camels to California* (Palo Alto: Stanford University Press, 1950).

4. Consult Maymie Krythe, *Port Admiral: Phineas Banning* (San Francisco: California Historical Society, 1957).

5. A popularized biography of Murieta is Walter Noble Burns, *The Robin Hood of El Dorado* (New York: Coward-McCann, 1932); also, see Ben C. Truman, *Life, Adventures and Capture of Tiburcio Vásquez* (Los Angeles Star, 1874); and Ernest May, "Tiburcio Vásquez," *Quarterly of the Historical Society of Southern California*, XXIX (Sept. 1947), 123–135.

CHAPTER FIVE

1. Consult John W. Robinson, *Los Angeles in Civil War Days* (Los Angeles: Dawson's Book Shop, 1977); and Helen B. Walters, "Confederates in Southern Califonia," *Historical Society of Southern Cali-*

fornia Quarterly, XXXV (1953), 41–54. See also William B. Rice, *The Los Angeles Star, 1851–1890* (Berkeley: University of California Press, 1947).

2. The standard authority is Glenn S. Dumke, *The Boom of the Eighties in Southern California* (San Marino: Huntington Library, 1944).

3. Consult John E. Baur, *Health Seekers of Southern California* (San Marino: Huntington Library, 1959).

CHAPTER SIX

1. A useful survey of agricultural development is Lawrence J. Jelinek, *Harvest Empire: A History of California Agriculture* (San Francisco: Boyd & Fraser, 1979).

2. See Charles Dwight Willard, *The Free Harbor Contest at Los Angeles* (Los Angeles: Kingsley, Barnes & Neuner, 1899).

3. *New West Magazine* (June 16, 1980), p. 46, repeats the same allegations that were rampant during the Owens Valley controversy. Consult W. A. Chalfant, *The Story of Inyo* (Chicago: privately printed, 1922); Frank M. Keffer, *History of the San Fernando Valley* (Glendale: Stillman Printing Co., 1934); and *Report of the Aqueduct Investigation Board to the City of Los Angeles* (Los Angeles: 1912). A summary is in W. W. Robinson, *The Story of San Fernando Valley* (Los Angeles: Title Insurance and Trust Co., 1961).

4. The latest work on the Owens Valley difficulties appears in Abraham Hoffman's *Vision or Villainy: Origins of the Owens Valley–Los Angeles Water Controversy* (College Station: Texas A&M University Press, 1981); and William L. Kahrl, "The Politics of California Water: Owens Valley and the Los Angeles Aqueduct, 1900–1927," *California Historical Quarterly*, LV (1976), 2–25 and 98–120. See also Remi Nadeau, *The Water Seekers* (Garden City, N.Y.: Doubleday, 1950).

CHAPTER SEVEN

1. Haynes and his wife, Dora, bequeathed a perpetual family trust for civic betterment, known today as the Haynes Foundation. Haynes served as the city's water and power commissioner from 1921 to 1937. See John Anson Ford, *Thirty Explosive Years in Los Angeles County* (San Marino: Huntington Library, 1961), 91.

2. Regarding the *Times,* consult Robert Gottlieb and Irene Wolt, *Thinking Big: The Story of the Los Angeles Times* (New York: Putnam, 1977); David Halberstam, *The Powers That Be* (New York: Knopf,

1979); and Richard C. Miller, "Otis and His *Times*" (Ph.D. dissertation, University of California, Berkeley, 1961). On the bombing of the *Times*, consult W. W. Robinson, *Bombs and Bribery: The Story of the McNamara and Darrow Trials* (Los Angeles: Dawson's Bookstore, 1969); and Adela Rogers St. Johns, *Final Verdict* (Garden City, N.Y.: Doubleday, 1962).

3. Wartime planning is described in Martin J. Schiesl, "City Planning and the Federal Government in World War II: The Los Angeles Experience," *California History*, LIX (Summer 1980), 126–143.

4. United States Works Progress Administration, Writer's Program, *Los Angeles: A Guide to the City and Its Environs* (New York: Hastings House, 1941), 277.

5. For a revisionist interpretation, see Frank W. Viehe, "The Recall of Mayor Frank L. Shaw," *California History*, LIX (Winter 1980), 290–305.

CHAPTER EIGHT

1. About Lummis, see Edwin Bingham, *Charles F. Lummis, Editor of the Southwest* (San Marino: Huntington Library, 1955); Dudley Gordon, *Charles F. Lummis, Crusader in Corduroy* (Los Angeles: Cultural Assets Press, 1972); and Turbese Lummis Fisk, *Charles F. Lummis, the Man and His West* (Norman: University of Oklahoma Press, 1975).

2. Consult Christine Sterling, *Olvera Street, Its History and Restoration* (Los Angeles: Adobe Studios, 1933) and Forman Brown, *Olvera Street and the Ávila Adobe* (Los Angeles: Dobe Dollar Bookstore, 1930).

3. Lately Thomas, *The Vanishing Evangelist* (New York: Viking, 1959).

4. See Edwin Cawston, *Ostriches and Ostrich Farming* (Los Angeles: Bentley & Sutton, 1887) as well as Nelson F. Johnson, *How Wild Animals Are Trained: Life of Al G. Barnes, World's Greatest Wild Animal Trainer* (Seattle: Ives, 1914); and Dave Robeson, *Al G. Barnes, Master Showman* (Caldwell, Idaho: Caxton Printers, 1933). Manuscripts and photos are in the Stonehouse Collection, Huntington Library, San Marino, Calif.

5. Security First National Bank, *Monthly Summary of Business Conditions* (July 31, 1979), 1–2.

6. Charles Champlin, "The Cultural Community: Building of Foundations," *Los Angeles Times*, Dec. 30, 1979.

7. *Los Angeles Times*, April 2, 1980.

CHAPTER NINE

1. Consult Robert Conot, *Rivers of Blood, Years of Darkness* (New York: Bantam Books, 1967) as well as Jerry Cohen and William Murphy, *Burn Baby Burn: The Los Angeles Race Riot, August, 1965)* (New York: Dutton, 1966). Also, see "Violence in the City," *A Report by the Governor's Commission on Los Angeles: The McCone Commission Hearings* (Sacramento: State Printing Office, 1965). Regarding the Los Angeles black community, a good start is Lawrence B. de Graff, "Negro Migration to Los Angeles, 1930 to 1950" (Ph.D. dissertation, University of California, Los Angeles, 1962). See also de Graff's "The City of Black Angels: Emergence of the Los Angeles Ghetto, 1890–1930, *Pacific Historical Review,* XXXIX (1970), 323–352. More general is Rudolph Lapp, *Afro-Americans in California* (San Francisco: Boyd & Fraser, 1979).

2. Quoted in Albert Camarillo, *Chicanos in a Changing Society: From Mexican Pueblos to American Barrios...* (Cambridge, Mass.: Harvard University Press, 1980), 189. See also Matt S. Meier and Feliciano Rivera, *The Chicanos: A History of Mexican Americans* (New York: Hill & Wang, 1972); Mark Reisler, *By the Sweat of Their Brow* (Westport, Conn.: Greenwood, 1976); and Richard Griswold del Castillo, *The Los Angeles Barrio, 1850–1890* (Berkeley: University of California Press, 1980).

3. *Los Angeles Times,* April 9, 1979, and April 13, 1980.

4. About the *pachuco* and zoot-suit phenomena, see Fritz Redl, "Zoot Suits: An Interpretation," *Survey Midmonthly,* LXXIX (Oct. 1943), 259–262; Ralph H. Turner and Samuel J. Surace, "Zoot Suiters and Mexicans: Symbols in Crowd Behavior," *American Journal of Sociology,* LVI (1956), 14–24, and Marilyn Domer, "Zoot Suit Riot" (M.A. thesis, Claremont Graduate School, 1955). Consult also Ralph S. Banay, "A Psychiatrist Looks at the Zoot Suit," *Probation,* XII (Feb. 1944), 81–85; and Carey McWilliams, "Los Angeles, Pachuco Gangs," *New Republic,* CVIII (1943), 818–820.

5. *City of Los Angeles* v. *Superior Court,* 51 Cal. 2d. 857 (1959) is described in William W. Clary, *History of the Law Firm of O'Melveny & Myers, 1885–1965* (Los Angeles: privately printed, 1966), 621.

6. Interview in *Los Angeles Times,* March 31, 1980. The wartime experiences of the Japanese appear in Donald and Nadine Hata, *Japanese Americans and World War II* (St. Charles, Mo.: Forum Press, 1974).

7. Regarding the Jews, see Max Vorspan, *History of the Jews of Los Angeles* (San Marino: Huntington Library, 1970).

8. The 1871 Chinese massacre is treated in William R. Locklear, "The Celestials and the Angels: A Study of the Anti-Chinese Movement in Los Angeles to 1882," *Southern California Quarterly,* XLII (Sept. 1960), 239–250, 253–254. As to the Italians, see Andrew Rolle, *The Immigrant Upraised: Italian Adventurers and Colonists in an Expanding America* (Norman: University of Oklahoma Press, 1968).

9. *Los Angeles Times,* April 9, 1979; April 13, 1980; Jan. 25, 1981.

10. For a recent article on the Chinese, see David R. Chan, "The Chinese Experience in Los Angeles," *Chinese Historical Society Bulletin* XV (March 1980), 3–16.

CHAPTER TEN

1. The 1930s through the 1950s have been described in John Anson Ford, *Thirty Explosive Years in Los Angeles County* (San Marino: Huntington Library, 1961), *passim.*

2. Security First National Bank, *Monthly Summary of Business Conditions* (Aug. 31, 1979), 1–2.

3. Christopher Rand, *Los Angeles: The Ultimate City* (New York: Oxford University Press, 1967), 32.

4. For a critique of local architecture, see Reyner Banham, *Los Angeles: The Architecture of Four Ecologies* (London: Penguin, 1971); see also David Gebhard and Harriette von Breton, *L.A. in the Thirties* (Santa Barbara: Peregrine Smith, 1975). Gebhard has also published "The Spanish Colonial Revival in Southern California, 1895–1930," *Journal of the Society of Architectural History* (May 1967), 131–147; and, with Robert Winter, *A Guide to Architecture in Southern California* (Los Angeles: County Museum of Art, 1965) and a second edition (Santa Barbara: Peregrine Smith, 1977). A good summary is Brendan Gill, "Reflections on Los Angeles Architecture," *New Yorker* (Sept. 15, 1980), 109 ff.

5. *Los Angeles Times,* Feb. 4, 1970.

6. See John L. Chapman, *Incredible Los Angeles* (New York: Harper & Row, 1967); Alison Lurie, *The Nowhere City* (New York: Coward-McCann, 1966); and John Halpern, *Los Angeles: Improbable City* (New York: Dutton, 1979).

7. In 1978 each policeman had to deal with an average of 33 criminal offenses. The robbery rate that year was 627.2 per 100,000 while the assaults carried out were 607.8 per 100,000. The rape rate that year was 90.5 per 100,000 inhabitants. See *Los Angeles Times,* Nov. 16 and 20, 1980; Jan. 2 and 22, 1981.

8. Quoted in Richard Reeves, "Vulnerable," *New Yorker* (Nov. 5, 1979), 154.

9. During the 1981 bicentennial celebrations the focus tended toward entertainment, with the festivities overwhelmingly self-congratulatory. Angelenos turned over historical analysis of their past to media writers and performers for the most part, despite the dedication of a small group of professional historians.

SUGGESTED READINGS

GENERAL LITERATURE includes: U.S. Works Progress Administration, Writer's Program, *Los Angeles: A Guide to the City and Its Environs* (rev. ed., New York: Hastings House, 1951); *Bill Murphy's Guidebook: Los Angeles and Southern California* (Garden City, N.Y.: Doubleday, 1962); Glenn Cunningham, ed., *Day Tours: Geographic Journeys in the Los Angeles Area* (Los Angeles: Pacific Books, 1964); California State Division of Beaches and Parks, *California Historical Landmarks* (Sacramento: State Printing Office, 1964); W. W. Robinson, *Panorama: A Picture History of Southern California* (Los Angeles: Title Insurance and Trust Co., 1953), and the same author's *Los Angeles from the Days of the Pueblo* (San Francisco: California Historical Society, 1959) and his *What They Say about the Angels* (Pasadena: Val Trefz Press, 1942). See also James M. Guinn, *A History of California and an Extended History of Los Angeles* (3 vols., Los Angeles: Historic Record Co., 1915); Boyle Workman, *The City That Grew* (Los Angeles: Southland, 1935); Remi A. Nadeau, *City-Makers* (Garden City, N.Y.: Doubleday, 1948); Harry Carr, *Los Angeles, City of Dreams* (New York: Grosset & Dunlap, 1949); Joseph G. Layne, *Books of the Los Angeles District* (Los Angeles: Dawson's Book Shop, 1950), a bibliography. See also R. Mayer, *Los Angeles, A Chronological and Documentary History* (Oceana, n.d.).

Helpful to an understanding of southern California's aborigines are Robert F. Heizer and Mary Ann Whipple, *California Indians: A Source Book* (Berkeley: University of California Press, 1951), and C. Hart Merriam, *Studies of California Indians* (Berkeley: University of California Press, 1955). Publications of the Southwest Museum, especially its journal *Masterkey*, are also useful.

Richard Henry Dana's 1840 minor classic, *Two Years Before the Mast* (Los Angeles: Ward Ritchie Press, 1964), reflects the pastoral life that he witnessed. Iris Higbie Wilson's *William*

Wolfskill, 1798–1866: Frontier Trapper to California Ranchero (Glendale: Arthur H. Clark, 1965) deals with one of the early pioneers of Los Angeles. On Fort Moore, see Andrew F. Rolle, "New Flag over Fort Moore," *Westways*, XLVIII (Sept. 1956), 4–5. Robert G. Cleland's *The Cattle on a Thousand Hills* (San Marino: Huntington Library, 1941) gives a good account of Los Angeles's transition from Mexican to American society.

Other books that continue the same story include George H. Banning, *Six Horses* (New York: Century, 1930); Charles B. Glasscock, *Lucky Baldwin: The Story of an Unconventional Success* (Indianapolis: Bobbs-Merrill, 1933); and Susanna Bryant Dakin, *A Scotch Paisano: Hugo Reid's Life in California* (Berkeley: University of California Press, 1939).

The development of municipalities around Los Angeles is told in W. W. Robinson, *Ranchos Become Cities* (Pasadena: San Pasqual Press, 1939). For the Civil War period, see Percival J. Cooney, "Southern California in Civil War Days," *Historical Society of Southern California Annual*, XIII (1924), 54–68, and Maymie Krythe, *Port Admiral: Phineas Banning* (San Francisco: California Historical Society, 1957). A standard work is Glenn S. Dumke, *The Boom of the Eighties in Southern California* (San Marino: Huntington Library, 1944); also, see Ludwig Louis Salvator, *Los Angeles in the Sunny Seventies* (Los Angeles: Bruce McCallister & Jake Zeitlin, 1929) for local color. A delicious account of life on a sheep ranch is Sarah Bixby Smith, *Adobe Days* (Cedar Rapids, Iowa: Torch Press, 1925). Harris Newmark's *Sixty Years in Southern California* (New York: Putnam, 1926) deals with economic development, as do J. A. Graves, *My Seventy Years in California, 1857–1929* (Los Angeles: Times-Mirror Co., 1929) and his *California Memories* (Los Angeles: Times-Mirror, Co., 1930).

Charting the expansion of a town to a city is Oscar O. Winther, "The Rise of Metropolitan Los Angeles, 1870–1900," *Huntington Library Quarterly*, X (1947), 391–405. See also John E. Baur, *Health Seekers of Southern California, 1870–1900* (San Marino: Huntington Library, 1959). The further growth of Los Angeles is examined in W. W. Robinson, *Los Angeles from the Days of the Pueblo* (San Francisco: California Historical Society, 1959) and Remi Nadeau, *City-Makers* (Garden City, N.Y.: Doubleday, 1948), as well as the latter's *Los Angeles: From*

Mission to Modern City (New York: David McKay, 1960). A useful little volume is W. W. Robinson, *Los Angeles: A Profile* (Norman: University of Oklahoma Press, 1968). Sketchy, popularized, and impressionistic is John D. Weaver, *El Pueblo Grande* (Los Angeles: Ward Ritchie Press, 1973). More substantial is Richard Lillard, *Eden in Jeopardy* (New York: Alfred A. Knopf, 1966).

Dated but still useful is the economic history by Robert Glass Cleland and Osgood Hardy, *The March of Industry* (Los Angeles: Powell, 1929). For the development of oil, farming, and manufacturing, see Carey McWilliams, *California: The Great Exception* (New York: A. A. Wyn, 1950); his *Southern California Country: An Island on the Land* (New York: Duell, Sloan & Pearce, 1946); and his *Factories in the Fields* (Boston: Little, Brown, 1939). Useful as to dispersal of the city is Robert M. Fogelson, *The Fragmented Metropolis: Los Angeles, 1850–1930* (Cambridge, Mass.: Harvard University Press, 1967).

Regarding the oil industry, consult Walker A. Tompkins, *Little Giant of Signal Hill* (Englewood Cliffs, N.J.: Prentice Hall, 1964); and W. H. Hutchinson, *Oil, Land and Politics: The California Career of Thomas Robert Bard* (Norman: University of Oklahoma Press, 1965).

The building of the city's controversial first water system is treated in Abraham Hoffman's *Vision or Villainy: Origins of the Owens Valley–Los Angeles Water Controversy* (College Station: Texas A&M University Press, 1981); and Remi Nadeau's *The Water Seekers* (Garden City, N.Y.: Doubleday, 1948). Regarding early banking, see Robert Glass Cleland and Frank B. Putnam, *Isaias W. Hellman and the Farmers and Merchants Bank* (San Marino: Huntington Library, 1965).

Construction of Los Angeles harbor is discussed in Charles A. Matson's *Building a World Gateway* (Los Angeles: Pacific Era Publishers, 1945). Spencer Crump, *Ride the Big Red Cars: How Trolleys Helped Build Southern California* (Los Angeles: Crest Publications, 1962), and Mitchell Gordon, *Sick Cities* (New York: Macmillan, 1963) explain the construction and destruction of Los Angeles's only truly effective public transport system, the old Pacific Electric Railway network.

Concerning the reform movement in California prior to World War I, consult George E. Mowry, *The California Progres-*

sives (Berkeley: University of California Press, 1951). On writing in southern California, see Franklin D. Walker, *A Literary History of Southern California* (Berkeley: University of California Press, 1950).

Regarding journalism in Los Angeles, consult William B. Rice, *History of the Los Angeles Star* (Berkeley: University of California Press, 1947). Little has been written about the labor history of Los Angeles: consult, however, Grace H. Stimson, *Rise of the Labor Movement in Los Angeles, 1875–1912* (Berkeley: University of California Press, 1955); and Louis B. and Richard Perry, *A History of the Los Angeles Labor Movement, 1911–1941* (Berkeley: Institute of Industrial Relations, University of California, 1963).

Developments in higher education are charted in Manuel P. Servín and Iris H. Wilson, *Southern California and Its University* (Los Angeles: Ward Ritchie Press, 1969); and Andrew Rolle, *Occidental College: The First Seventy-Five Years* (Los Angeles: Anderson, Ritchie & Simon, 1962). Concerning UCLA, see Ernest Carroll Moore's *I Helped Make a University* (Los Angeles: Anderson, Ritchie & Simon, 1952).

Regarding the cinema in Hollywood there are many books, including Edward Wagenknecht, *The Movies in the Age of Innocence* (Norman: University of Oklahoma Press, 1962).

Carey McWilliams gives the reader some of the best analyses of occultism and faddism in his already mentioned *Southern California Country* and *California: The Great Exception;* also consult appropriate excerpts in Edmund Wilson, *The American Earthquake* (Garden City, N.Y.: Doubleday, 1958).

A life of Aimee Semple McPherson is Nancy Barr Mavity, *Sister Aimée* (Garden City, N.Y.: Doubleday, 1931); another work about her is Lately Thomas, *The Vanishing Evangelist* (New York: Viking, 1959). For loyal adulation of a controversial facet of southern California's commercialized "cemetery culture," see Adela Rogers St. Johns, *First Step Up Toward Heaven* (Englewood Cliffs, N.J.: Prentice-Hall, 1959), which may be contrasted with Evelyn Waugh's satire, *The Loved One* (Boston: Little, Brown, 1948), and Aldous Huxley's earlier, but equally acid, novel, *After Many a Summer Dies the Swan* (New York: Harper & Row, 1939), both also available in paperback editions.

John Fante's *Ask the Dust* (Harrisburg, Pa.: Stackpole, 1940) is a novel set on Bunker Hill. It roams far beyond such books as Allison Lurie's *The Nowhere City* (New York: Avon paperback, 1975) and resembles Robert Towne's script for *Chinatown,* a TV film and movie. A lampooning of southern California is Cynthia Lindsay, *The Natives Are Restless* (Philadelphia: J. B. Lippincott, 1960), also available in an inexpensive paper edition. Another examination of the southern part of the state is Jessamyn West's *South of the Angels* (New York: Harcourt, Brace & World, 1960). See also Jack Smith, *The Big Orange* (Los Angeles: 1976).

Population statistics form part of the annual reports of the Southern California Research Council. These are prepared by business executives and Occidental and Pomona college economists. The publications of the Haynes Foundation regarding municipal matters are also useful. The newsletters of the Security First National Bank provide considerable information regarding economy and society. See, too, files of the *Los Angeles Times.* Useful but dated are Eshref Shevsky and M. Williams, *The Social Areas of Los Angeles* (Berkeley: University of California Press, 1949), as well as George W. Bemis and Nancy Basche, *Los Angeles County as an Agency of Municipal Government* (Los Angeles: Haynes Foundation, 1947).

Useful guides to the city's resources are Judson A. Grenier, ed., *A Guide to Historic Places in Los Angeles County* (Dubuque, Iowa: Kendall Hunt, 1978); David Gebhard and Harriette von Breton, *Los Angeles in the Thirties* (Santa Barbara: Peregrine Smith, 1975); David Gebhard and Robert Winter, *A Guide to Architecture in Los Angeles and Southern California* (Santa Barbara: Peregrine Smith, 1977) as well as Andrew Rolle, *Los Angeles: A Student's Guide to Localized History* (New York: Columbia University Press, 1965). Over a hundred essays have been gathered together by John and La Ree Caughey in *Los Angeles: Biography of a City* (Berkeley: University of California Press, 1976). See also Doyce B. Nunis, Jr., ed., *Los Angeles and Its Environs in the Twentieth Century: A Bibliography* (Los Angeles: Ward Ritchie Press, 1973). Art Seidenbaum, *Los Angeles Two Hundred . . .* (New York: Abrams, 1980) is primarily a picture book that celebrates the city's bicentennial.

Before visiting California Hall at the Los Angeles County

Museum, consult *A Guide and Catalogue of California Hall* (Los Angeles County Museum, 1965), edited by Russell E. Belous and Burton A. Reiner. Consult the useful *Los Angeles: An Instructional Resource Guide* (1980) published by the Office of the Los Angeles County Superintendent of Schools to celebrate the bicentennial of the city. See the list of monuments and historic sites on p. 176. Finally, consult Julius Shulman, *The Best of Los Angeles: A Discriminating Guide* (Los Angeles: Rosebud Books, 1980).

INDEX